"Creat
can solve
any problem...
the creative act,
the defeat
o f habit by originality,
overcomes
everything."

GEORGE LOIS

1959
DOYLE DANE BERNBACH

1964
PAPERT KOENIG LOIS

1970
LOIS HOLLAND CALLAWAY

1978
LOIS PITTS GERSHON

1985
LOIS/USA

2002
GOOD KARMA CREATIVE

"To sin by silence when they should protest makes cowards of men."

ABRAHAM LINCOLN

In 1951, I was drafted into the army. My first day at Camp Gordon in the deep Jim Crow South, roll call at 6.00 a.m. went like this: "Jones!" "Right chere!" "Jackson!" "Right chere!" "Longstreet!" "Right chere!" "Lois!" "Yo!" When we were dismissed, a red-faced major confronted me: "What's with the 'Yo' soldier?!" "Answering roll call, sir." "Why the 'Yo' soldier?" "Well, the Southern boys all say 'Right chere'—but I'm from New York, so I say Yo!" The major leaned in, and between gritted teeth said, "Oh, another Noo Yawk, Jew Fag, Niggah lover!" I braced myself, and my exact reply to him was, "Go fuck yourself, sir!" I was given 14 weeks company punishment, and shipped off to Korea. (Thank you, Abraham Lincoln!)

Being raised as a Greek kid in a racist Irish neighborhood and my experiences as a young G.I. fighting in an army committing genocide on an Asian culture led me, indeed forced me, when I came home, to live a life as a graphic communicator determined to awaken, to disturb, to protest, to instigate, to provoke.

At every opportunity, I have attempted to speak truth to power — to fight the "authorities," unjust courts, police harassment, the consistent loss of our civil liberties, a government that benefits the wealthy at the expense of the poor and powerless, and America's unending wars—by creating graphic imagery and organizing battles against ethnic, religious, and racial injustice, always standing against a conservative, indoctrinated, and racist society, and playing a conscious role…as a cultural provocateur.

To me, a true creative spirit means to fight the good fight, always rejecting Con…and creating Icon.

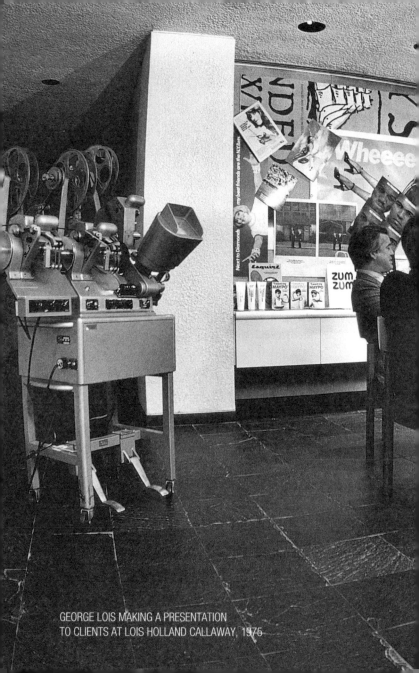

GEORGE LOIS MAKING A PRESENTATION
TO CLIENTS AT LOIS HOLLAND CALLAWAY, 1975

1.
There are only four types of person you can be. Identify yourself:

1

Very bright, Industrious

(You're perfect.)

2 Very bright, Lazy

(A damn shame.)

3 Stupid, Lazy

(You'll just sit on your ass, so you're a wash.)

4 Stupid, Industrious

(Oh, oh, you're dangerous.)

**If you're a number 1 or a 2,
you'll get a lot out of this book.
If you're a number 3 or 4,
why are you reading this book?**

2.

"I yam what I yam, an dat's all I yam, I'm Popeye the Sailor Man."

Whether you're male, female, black, Hispanic,
Native American, Asian, ethnic, or gay (and wherever
you work), you are who you are, and that's what
you are – and be damn proud of it.
Don't change your name, don't change your
accent, don't change your heritage,
don't denigrate a humble upbringing.
Be true to yourself and you'll
ring true to the world.

3.
Follow your bliss.

Reflecting on Sinclair Lewis' novel *Babbitt* (1922),
Joseph Campbell, the profoundly wise American mythologist
and philosopher said, "Remember the last line?
'I have never done a thing that I wanted to do in all my life.'
That is a man who never followed his bliss."
With this statement, Campbell nailed the secret of living
a joyous, fruitful, and successful life:
Follow your bliss. That which you love, you must spend
your life doing, as passionately and as perfectly
as your heart, mind, and instincts allow. And the sooner
you identify that bliss, which surely resides
in the soul of most human beings, the greater your chance
of a truly successful life.

4.
My Anti-Slogan: "George, be careful!"

Looking up from my crib on a dark and stormy night, God commanded: "George, be careful." (I remember it well.) My earliest childhood recollections were punctuated by three words (in Greek) from the lips of my mother, Vasilike Thanasoulis Lois: "George, be careful." They have been a refrain throughout my life – a sincere admonition from the lips of people who have always meant well but never fathomed my attitude towards life and work. In the act of creativity, being careful guarantees sameness and mediocrity, which means your work will be invisible.

Better to be reckless than careful.
Better to be bold than safe.
Better to have your work seen and remembered, or you've struck out.

There is no middle ground.

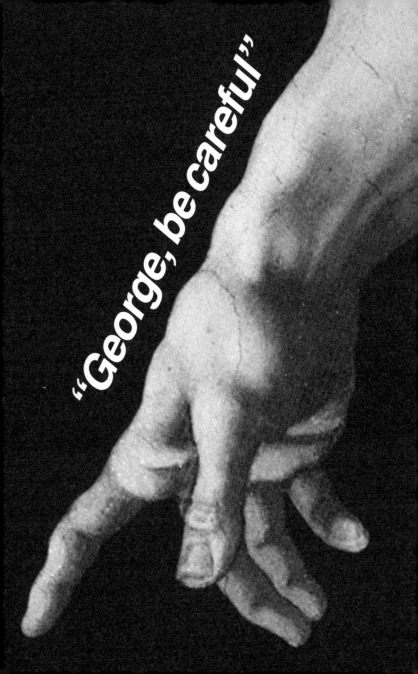

5.
When I was 14, I had an epiphany that inspired my life. Maybe it can be yours!

In the early twentieth century, Kazimir Malevich changed the future of modern art and led the Russian avant-garde into pure abstraction. Thirty years later, as a freshman at the High School of Music & Art in Manhattan, I was asked to create similar compositions every day in a basic design course. The more we ripped off a Malevich, (or Klee, Bayer, Albers, or Mondrian), the better Mr. Patterson liked it. Bo-r-r-ring!

In the last class of the year, when Mr. Patterson (sternly) once again asked us to create a design on 18 x 24 illustration board using only rectangles and called it a final exam, I made my move. As my 26 classmates worked furiously, cutting and pasting, I sat motionless. Mr. Patterson, eyeballing me, was doing a slow burn as he walked up and down the classroom, peering over the shoulder of each student. Time was up. Growing apoplectic as he stacked the final designs, he went to grab my completely empty board, when I thrust my arm forwards and interrupted him by casually signing "G. Lois" in the bottom left-hand corner. He was thunderstruck. I had "created" the ultimate 18 x 24 rectangle design!

I had taught myself that my work had to be fresh, different, seemingly outrageous. From then on, I understood that nothing is as exciting as an idea.

KAZIMIR MALEVICH,
1915

GEORGE LOIS,
1945

GEORGE LOIS, 1991

6.
All the tools in the world are meaningless without an essential idea.

An artist, or advertising man, or anyone involved in a creative industry (or even noncreative professions such as a doctor, lawyer, electrician, factory worker, or president) without an idea, is unarmed. In the graphic arts, when that original idea springs out of a creative's head and intuitions, the mystical and artful blending (or even juxtaposition) of concept, image, words, and art can lead to magic, where one and one can indeed be three.

7.
But creating ideas without a work ethic to follow through is inconceivable to me.

If you don't burn out at the end of each day, you're a bum! People watching me work ask me all the time why I'm not burnt out, how (especially now at my age) I manage to keep going. The fact is, I'm totally burnt out at the end of each day because I've given myself totally to my work – mentally, psychologically, physically. When I head home at night I can't see straight. But I love that feeling of utter depletion: It is an ecstatic sense of having committed myself to the absolute limit. But after recharging at night, I'm ready to go the next morning. Isn't that what life is all about?

8.
Always go for The Big Idea.

The Big Idea in advertising sears the virtues of a product into a viewer's brain and heart, resulting in a sales explosion. To be a master communicator, words and images must catch people's eyes, penetrate their minds, warm their hearts, and cause them to act! Read just one of the books I've written and there are hundreds of examples of my ad campaigns that prove what I've always insisted: great advertising, in and of itself, becomes a benefit of the product. As an entrepreneur; in a new business start-up; in *any* creative industry – always go for The Big Idea.

9.
All creativity should communicate in a nanosecond.

Certainly, the greatest advertising, poster, packaging, magazine cover, book cover, logotype design, etc. needs to connect instantly with the human brain and heart to remain memorable. This minimalist ad I created in 1960 for Coldene cough syrup was a visual atom bomb when the readers of *Life* and *Look* opened their pages. The pre-feminism repartee of the sleepy couple in bed being awakened by their coughing kid was the talk of the ad world when it hit the newsstands. No product, no logo, no diagram.

In the business world, long, drawn-out, uncommunicative, fumbling presentations are the norm. As you read this, thousands of speeches, powerpoint presentations, and off-the-cuff talks are leaving audiences catatonic. Understand this: If you can't express your thinking concisely and surprisingly – and literally communicate it visually in a nanosecond – it's not a Big Idea.

"John,
is
that
Billy
coughing?"

"Get up
and
give
him
some
Coldene."

10.
My first commandment:
The word comes first, *then* the visual.

When young art directors ask me to reveal my "formula" for creating
advertising, I answer...start with the word! This advice, with
a biblical reference, is carved in stone – my first commandment.
Art directors, presumed by many to be illiterate, are expected
to think visually – and most do. They sift through magazines to find
visuals, however disjointed and inappropriate, to help them
"get started." Most art directors, unfortunately, do not sit and try to
write the idea: they usually wait with their thumbs up their
ass for a writer to furnish the words, which usually are not visually
pregnant. By contrast, a handful of great art directors are
authors of some of the finest headlines in advertising – or they work
intimately with gifted writers as they conjure concepts
together. Conversely, even when a writer works on his own, his words
must lend themselves to visual excitement – because
a big campaign idea can only be expressed in words that
absolutely bristle with visual possibilities, leading
to words and visual imagery working in perfect synergy.

If you're an art director, heed my words: Each ad,
TV spot, and campaign is in *your* hands – it's your baby.
If you're a copywriter, on the other hand, you *must*
work with a talented visual communicator!

JOHN 1:1
KING JAMES BIBLE

IN
THE
BEGINNING
WAS
THE WORD

11.
"I'm sorry I could not have written a shorter letter, but I didn't have the time."

Abraham Lincoln.

Not too long after U.S. President Abraham Lincoln delivered the iconic wartime Gettysburg Address of 1863 in under three minutes and in just 10 sentences (272 words he had written and rewritten and agonized over), he wrote a long letter, in *minuscule* handwriting, to a friend. The apology above, that he didn't have the time to contemplate, correct, and edit his letter, is the most lucid lesson in good writing I've ever read. Keep it short, informative, concise, and literary, where every single word counts. But remember: It's not how short you make it; it's how you make it short.

Think long. Write short.

12.
"Words can not express how articulate I feel."

It never fails. When I lecture at colleges and design conferences all over the world, I'm usually asked the question, "Is it important to be able to speak well in the creative field? Don't most 'artists' have a problem communicating on their feet?" Huh? The response, in my thick Noo Yawk accent, flies out of my mouth: "Words can not express how articulate I feel." Which is my wise-guy way of saying, **if you can't passionately and succinctly explain your creative ideas, fuggedaboutit!**

13.
Don't expect a creative idea to pop out of your computer.

I've witnessed a myriad of creative "professionals" (as well as *all* design students) fishing on the computer, frantically looking, searching, praying, for an idea. Look deeply, deeply, into the screen – there's nothing there! Without a creative idea in your head, the computer is a mindless speed machine, producing tricks without substance, form without relevant content, or content without meaningful form. The capability of a computer to produce bells and whistles can *never* inspire the conception of a Big Idea.

So don't sit down at your computer until you've grasped a big concept, without a computer in sight.
You can't run until you can walk.

"Duh!"

A trend is always a trap.

Because advertising and marketing is an art, the solution to each
new problem or challenge should begin with a blank canvas
and an open mind, not with the nervous borrowings of other people's
mediocrities. That's precisely what "trends" are – a search
for something "safe" – and why a reliance on them leads to oblivion.
At the start of each new year, as the press scans the horizon
for newsworthy departures from the past, I'm usually asked by
reporters from America's news weeklies: "What do you
think the trends in advertising will be in the coming year?"
My answer is always identical to what I said the previous year:
"Beats the shit out of me. I'll know it when I do it."
Trends can tyrannize; trends are traps. In any creative industry,
the fact that others are moving in a certain
direction is always proof positive, at least to me, that
a *new* direction is the *only* direction.

15.
Creativity is not *created*, it is there for us to find – it is an act of *discovery*.

Great advertising comes down to The Big Idea, but I never create the ideas that characterize my work. I discover them – snared from the air as they float by me. (Michelangelo said that a sculpture is imprisoned in a block of marble, and only a great sculptor can set it free.) Sounds mystical, perhaps, but after doing the requisite homework to understand a product, its competitors, etc., ideas in advertising are ignited by the sparks and sounds of an understanding of 7,000 years of the history of mankind.

Plato defined "Idea" (*eidos*) as a mental image. I don't create that mental image in my head. I somehow see it in my mind's eye, floating by me, and I reach out and grab it. So if you're trying to achieve greatness in *any* creative industry, go out into the world and sail the ocean blue and live a life of discovery.

CHRISTOPHER COLUMBUS
SEBASTIANO DEL PIOMBO, 1520

16.
Why just be a *Creative Thinker*—when you can be a *Cultural Provocateur!*

Great graphic and verbal communication depends on understanding and adapting to the culture, anticipating the culture, criticizing changes in the culture, and helping to *change* the culture. Any entrepreneur, inventor, artist, graphic designer, adman, fashion designer, architect, editor, doctor, lawyer, politician—anyone who instinctively feels the way to go is against a conservative, indoctrinated society and bucks the trend, and who understands the zeitgeist of the time—has the passion and capability to become a *cultural provocateur*. So if you're a young person with an entrepreneurial spirit who aspires to succeed, not only in business, but in life, your mission is not to sedate, but to awaken, to disturb, to communicate, to command, to instigate, and even to *provoke*.

VINCENT VAN GOGH'S
PORTRAIT OF THE ARTIST, 1889
BY GEORGE LOIS, 2011

17.
A Big Idea can change world culture.

MTV, now regarded as a "sure thing from the start," was an abject failure after its first full year of operation. But in 1982 I got rock fans to phone their local cable operators and yell, *I want my MTV.* Overwhelmed, the operators called the Warner Amex cable-TV network and begged them to stop running my commercials because they didn't have an army of telephone operators to answer the calls, and Warner Amex immediately surrendered. MTV was alive and rockin.'

A few weeks before, when I had presented my campaign idea to their execs, they insisted that no rock star would assist MTV because music publishers feared the MTV concept would kill their business, record companies swore they would never produce music videos, advertisers considered it a joke, ad agency experts snickered, and cable operators scoffed. But with one pleading phone call to London, I convinced Mick Jagger to help (for no dough), and 20 years before the bad boy of rock became a knight of the realm, I anointed Sir Mick the patron saint of MTV. Within a few weeks of the premiere of Jagger picking up the phone and saying *I want my MTV*, every rock star in America was calling me, begging to scream *I want my MTV* to the world.

The lesson (which most ad agencies have never understood) is that **great advertising can perform a marketing miracle!**

18.

"There's a great solution, a Big Idea, buried in every assignment, whether for a new ad campaign, poster, brand name, letterhead, matchbook cover – even a number slapped on a building."

I once emphatically stated this to a class I was teaching.
A week later a real estate firm asked me to
design a logo for 20 Times Square. It was as if God was
telling me to put up or shut up. A multitude
of handsome logos have been designed over the centuries,
but they are what they are, certainly not a Big Idea.
Omigosh – how do you get a stunning idea for a logo for
20 Times Square?! I got it –
a 20, a multiplication sign, and a square!

I've always maintained that I never "create" an idea.
Getting a Big Idea is not an act of inspiration, but rather one of discovery (see 15).
My logo for 20 Times Square proved me right.

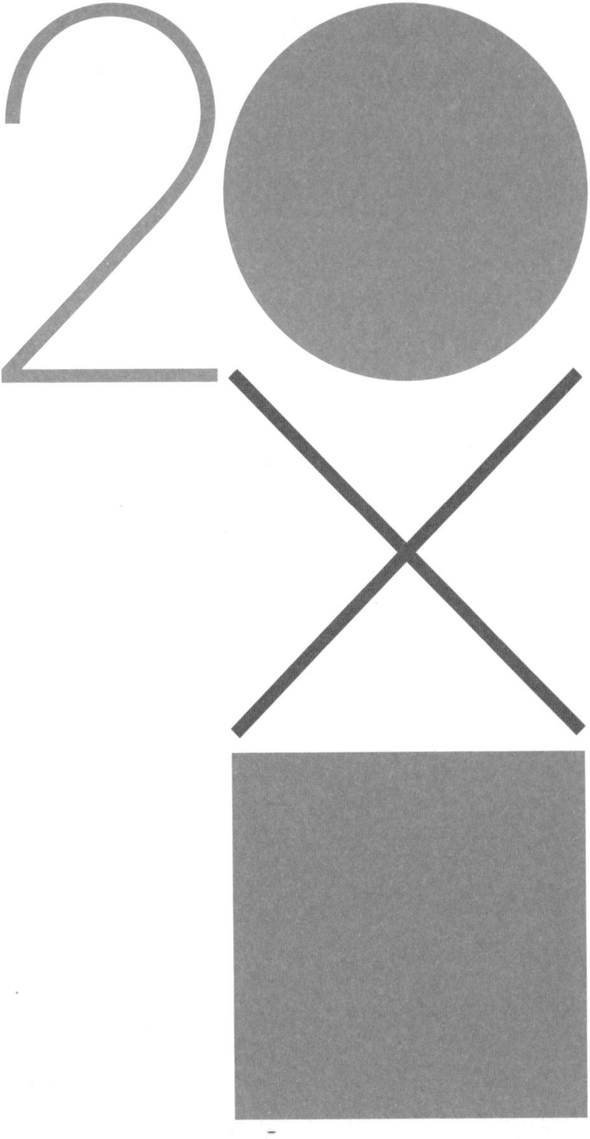

19.
You can be Cautious or you can be Creative (but there's no such thing as a Cautious Creative).

A creative thinker must be fearless.
If you're more tentative than decisive, if you're more
cautious than creative, you'll never be
an innovative business leader, and certainly not
a great visual communicator.
A Cautious Creative is an oxymoron.

20.
But always remember, you're trying to sell something. So ask for the sale!

We live in a timid age when students and young professionals are "taught" to believe that a commercial or an ad should not be seen or experienced as a commercial or an ad! But a great commercial or print advertisement *should* say, in-your-face, that this is a commercial message and that we're asking for the sale – not by pounding your head with a hammer, but by charming your ass off! People enjoy being sold products, and they fully understand that the art of selling is being done through the popular art form of advertising, but in answering research questions, most people will insist they *hate* advertising – trust me, **when it's done right, the cash registers ring.**

21.
"Advertising," I replied, "is Poison Gas!"

I once appeared on *The David Susskind Show*, a national talk show, to discuss advertising along with two CEOs of enormous ad agencies. Susskind's opening question was, "Gentlemen, what is advertising?" One of the gray suits tackled the question with a five-minute soliloquy like an emeritus professor in a college course on marketing. The second expert, clearly impressed, praised the summary as a succinct explanation of advertising. As I listened to these two good ol' Establishment boys, I sank into my chair and my eyes rolled with dismay. Susskind spotted me and said, "Why are you making those faces, George? Don't you *agree* with these gentlemen?" I leaned forwards and said, "I think these guys and me are in a different business." Susskind was titillated by my assuming the role of a provocateur. With relish, he asked me, "Well, what do *you* think advertising is?" "Advertising," I replied, "is poison gas. **It should bring tears to your eyes, unhinge your nervous system, and knock you out.**" My zinger, picked up by the wire services, was promptly printed in major newspapers across the nation. "Adman says Advertising is Poison Gas," they headlined. Plato and Spinoza may have been able to describe the reasoning process that should lead to great creativity, but they could never have created poison gas — or great advertising that bowls you over.

22.
You can *never* learn anything from a mistake!

Nobody's perfect. I always swing for homers, rather than lay down drag bunts. Trouble is, I sometimes strike out. I've had a few bombs, turkeys, misses (let's call them stinkers), but I contend to this day that they were all magnificent conceptions. A failure is supposed to give you pause, shake you up, humble you. But that would be the end of being a fearless, creative thinker.
**Onwards and upwards,
and never give your failures a second thought.**

23.
Never listen to music when you're trying to come up with a Big Idea.

Especially if you're a music lover. Music you consider great is involving and transformative, carrying you away – someplace you don't want to be when you need to solve a specific problem with a communicative idea.

24.
Drive your Big Idea to the very edge of the cliff (but if you go too far, it's a fiery death).

The point about unusual ideas has to be their proximity to madness.
Creativity is the ultimate adrenaline rush. If you have what
you consider a fantastic concept, you must drive it to the precipice.
If you don't take it to the edge, you've chickened out. And if
you want to do great advertising, you'll push your thought to the
very rim of insanity. To the very edge. But if you go too far,
you plunge to a fiery (and embarrassing) death.
So the real challenge is knowing when to stop. When you go too far,
lots of people think you're nuts. And for all you know,
they may be right. But you must take the risk.

25.
Reject Group Grope.

Think about this: Decisive, breakthrough creative decision-making
is almost always made by one, two, or possibly three minds
working in unison, take it or leave it. Collective thinking usually leads
to stalemate or worse. And the *smarter* the individuals in the
group, the harder it is to nail the idea. Certainly, in my experience
as a mass communicator and cultural provocateur, I know this
to be absolutely true: Group thinking and decision-making
results in group grope.

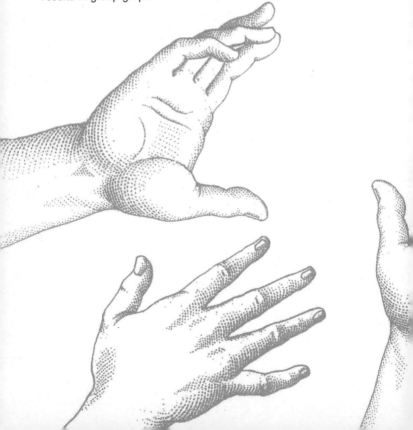

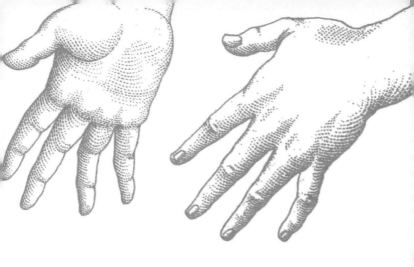

26.
Reject Analysis Paralysis.

Get the Big Idea, think it through – it all fits,
you know it's right, you know it's
ambitious and aggressive, it thrills every cell
in your body. Does it work in print? Yes.
Does it make a gangbuster TV spot? Yes. Put it
all on paper and sell it to your client.
Do not analyze it. Trust your gut. Trust your instincts.
In all creative decision-making, analysis
involves conjuring up not only the pros, but also those
hidden, spooky cons – and discussion
about the cons is, ipso facto, analysis paralysis.

Teamwork might work in building an Amish barn, but it can't create a Big Idea.

The accepted system for the creation of innovative thinking in a democratic environment is to work cooperatively in a teamlike ambience. Don't believe it. Whatever the creative industry, when you're confronted with the challenge of coming up with a Big Idea, always work with the most talented, innovative mind available. Hopefully...that's *you*. Avoid group grope (see 25) and analysis paralysis (see 26). The greatest innovative thinker of our age remains Apple cofounder Steve Jobs, a modern-day Henry Ford. Jobs was *not* a consensus builder but a dictator who listened to his own intuitions, blessed with an astonishing aesthetic sense. **Everybody believes in co-creativity – not me. Be confident of your own, edgy, solo talent.**

(Once you've got the Big Idea, that's where teamwork comes in – *selling* the Big Idea, *producing* the Big Idea, and bringing the Big Idea into *fruition*.)

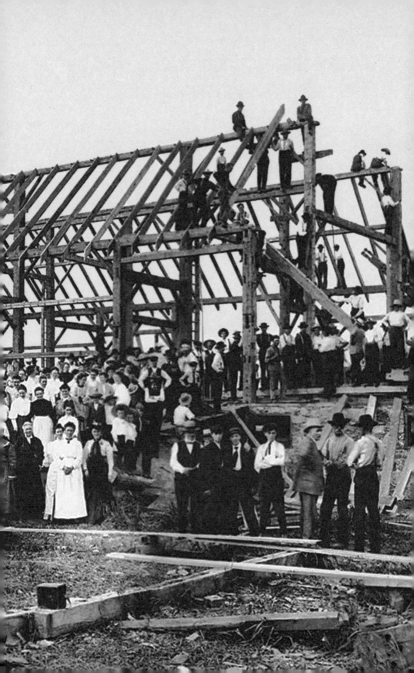

28.
To get that first big break, you can't just brag that you're "great."

To get that first stepping-stone job, you must *prove* you have talent. In the advertising world, you simply can't tell a pro that "I'm loaded with talent – just give me a chance." I wish I had a nickel for every young person who tried *that* line on me! You *must* show some examples of work that shows your real potential. You *must* have a portfolio, but you *can't* create one without some mentoring. Go to a school like the School of Visual Arts in New York City (staffed with working art directors and copywriters who are passionate about teaching) and take some conceptual design courses to build your portfolio, if only to prove to yourself that you truly have the right stuff.

IT'S NOT THE LIGHT AT THE END OF THE TUNNEL,
IT'S THE LIGHT WITHIN.
SCHOOL OF VISUAL ARTS

SUBWAY POSTER
FOR THE SCHOOL OF
VISUAL ARTS,
TONY PALLADINO, 1985

29.
Your portfolio should Ignite, Provoke, Shock, Kick Ass.

So many employers say that young people entering the business
are afraid to take chances, that they're as conservative as
the biggest stiffs in suits. But let's face it: That's the story of
mankind. We live in fear of life, in fear of work, in fear
of death. Students are taught to put together a "professional"
portfolio rather than one that boggles the mind as you
open it. The best creatives protest loudly that they want to see
kids take chances. *Then*, when they see a portfolio that's
a little off the wall, they say the kid lacks discipline, or that he
or she is a flake. It's confusing – kids are given no brave
direction. I spent my life listening to people say, "George, be careful"
(see 4). But being careful in creativity is synonymous
with doing uninspired work.

30.
I didn't have to be Jewish to love this campaign. So do what I did — get a job at a place that creates work that thrills you.

Witnessing the wit and power of the brilliant Levy's Rye campaign, when I was already making a name for myself in the design field while in my mid-20s, I knew Doyle Dane Bernbach, the pioneering creative agency of the twentieth century, was in my future. Bill Taubin, one of their ace art directors, and copywriter Dave Reider, a gemütlich pair if there ever was one, sold an ethnic product by tapping the warmth of human experience. In a series of posters, they depicted the reaction of a Native American, an Irish cop, a Chinese laundryman, a Catholic choirboy, a young African-American, even Buster Keaton, after biting a mouthful of a sandwich made with Levy's real Jewish rye; a mnemonic slogan and a mnemonic visual, synergistically blending and communicating in a nanosecond (see 64). In 1958, when I was hired by DDB's legendary boss, Bill Bernbach, this Greek "goy" sought out Taubin and Reider and genuflected, thanking them for the inspiration they instilled in my blooming career. No matter what field you're in, identify the revolutionary leaders, and create for those who have the capacity to thrill to *your* Big Ideas.

31.
Work is worship.

Working hard and doing great work is as imperative as breathing.
Creating great work warms the heart and enriches the soul.
Those of us lucky enough to spend our days doing something
we love, something we're good at, are rich. If you do not
work passionately (even furiously) at being the best in the world at
what you do, you fail your talent, your destiny, and your god.

32.
Throughout your career, be thrilled that you're doing work that you love (and getting a paycheck for it!).

Thomas Carlyle once wrote, "Blessed is he who has found his work;
let him ask no other blessedness." In the middle of my second
year at Pratt, my design teacher Herschel Levit threw me out of school
and got me a job with Reba Sochis' design studio. I remember
being amazed that I was working at what I always wanted to do — while
actually getting a paycheck for it — and I remember waiting in line
to cash my first week's paycheck for $45, astounded at my great luck.
Sixty years later, I still get that warmth at being rewarded for
doing what I love to do. Those of us who know that feeling should
remind ourselves of our good fortune when we drink our
coffee and head to work.

YOUNG MAN AT PRAYER (DETAIL)
HANS MEMLING, 1475

33.
Make your presence felt!

In 1952, a week back from the Korean War, I got a dream job
as a designer working with the iconic design master, William Golden,
at CBS television. On my second day, I was ready to present
my first design project to Golden. His secretary looked up at me from
a massive dictionary and smiled nervously when I asked to see
him. "Go ahead," she said, looking edgy. At the far end of a large room,
Bill Golden was at work at a drawing table. I walked in and waited
for him to look up, but he kept on working, his eyes riveted to
his layout. I cleared my throat. But Golden kept working. He knew
I was there and I knew he would never look up. A test of wills.

I walked back to Ms. Kerner. "May I borrow your dictionary?" I asked.
**Lifting the hulk from her desk, I went back into Golden's office,
stopped 3 feet from his desk, held the dictionary chest
high, and opened my hands – the massive book hit the floor with
an ear-splitting boom.** The pencil flew from Golden's hand and
his face jerked up. "Oh, George – can I help you?" he asked.
"Uh, yes, I'd like to show you an ad for the new *Gunsmoke* show."
I handed him the announcement ad and he said, "Good,
George. Excellent!" I took back my ad and returned the dictionary
to his stunned assistant.

The next morning I received a call from Cipe Pineles, Golden's wife,
a great editorial designer, and in a thick Viennese accent, she said
"G-G-Georges, you don't know me, but I'm Bill's vife, and I just vant to
congratulate you for not taking any of Bill's *bulll-shiit!*"

34.
Make one million dollars look like ten million dollars!

When I was a young art director at Doyle Dane Bernbach,
I never allowed anyone to present my work. Recognizing
the method to my madness, Bill Bernbach instructed his account
people to let the crazy young Greek do his own selling.
At a presentation to a major client, I was accompanied by two
account executives, the agency's media director,
and a senior copywriter, as well as Bill Bernbach and his partner
Ned Doyle, as I showed my work. The client loved
my campaign, and in the spirit of camaraderie, he asked the
account guys and the media director what they did
at the agency. Then he turned to me and asked, jokingly,
"And, George, what do *you* do?" "I make one million
dollars look like ten million dollars," I answered. Bernbach
and Doyle were absolutely floored. After that, everyone
at DDB called me "The Ten Million Dollar Man." Always sell
your work, not merely with total confidence,
but with the confidence of
a ten million dollar jewel thief.

35.
If it's a rush job, don't say No... say

NOW!

To work in the advertising business is to work in the land of perpetual deadlines, imposed and (I must confess) self-imposed. All my life I've always said "Now" instead of "No." Most creative industries have grueling work schedules and deadlines. No matter what kind of work you're in, do it fast, on-time, and do it perfectly.

36.
Most people work at *keeping* their job, rather than *doing* a good job.

If you're the former, you're leading a meaningless life.
If you're the latter, keep up the good work.

37.
Even a brilliant idea won't sell itself.

You're looking at Ron Holland, me, and Jim Callaway in 1967,
a few weeks after starting my second ad agency,
Lois Holland Callaway. As you can see, we're selling an ad campaign
to a new client (with gusto).

Always do three things when you present a Big Idea:
1. Tell them what they are going to see.
2. Show it to them.
3. Tell them, dramatically, what they just saw.

To sell work I could be proud of, I've had to rant, rave, threaten, shove,
push, cajole, persuade, wheedle, exaggerate, flatter, manipulate,
be obnoxious, be loud, occasionally lie, and always sell, *passionately!*
Abraham Lincoln once said: "When I hear a man preach,
I like to see him act as if he were fighting bees."

**To be a successful creative, be prepared for a lifetime
fighting bees (even if you sometimes get stung).**

38.
The ultimate act of Scholarship and Theater is the art of selling.

The most thrilling story of the marriage of expertise and style involves the art dealer, Lord Duveen. Finally receiving an audience from J.P. Morgan, the richest and most important collector of the twentieth century, the dandyish Duveen, with his tailcoat, spats, top hat, cane, and all, sashayed into the presence of Morgan in his luxurious mansion on Fifth Avenue. Without a greeting, Morgan pointed to five large vases on his marble floor and told Duveen that three were sixteenth-century Ming masterpieces, and the other two exact copies that had cost him a fortune to have made. He commanded Duveen to study the vases and tell him which were the copies and which were the invaluable originals. Lord Duveen strutted up to the vases, hardly glancing at them, raised his pearl-handled cane and, with two violent strokes, smashed two of them to smithereens. From that moment, every painting and art object that J.P. Morgan collected until the day he died, he bought from the great English salesman. Through ultimate confidence in his own abilities, **Duveen shows us that selling is truly an art that one must master to be successful.**

39.
Go head-to-head with a prospective client by hitting the nail on the head.

Al Neuharth, the chairman of *USA Today*, shouted,
"Lois, I'd have to ditch the largest ad agency
in America, and they run a ton of ads in Gannett's other papers.
What would people say if
I switched agencies?"

I politely replied, "They'd
probably say you're finally getting
your head screwed on straight!
You're doing pussy advertising now.
You ought to be doing triumphant
fucking advertising!"

A few months later Al Neuharth
told the world, "The man spoke my language...
I gave Lois my *USA Today* account –
and his advertising worked!"

**When a prospective client confronts you
with a do-or-die question –
nail him with the irreverent truth.**

40.
"Lois, you can't take yes for an answer!"

A QUOTE I HEARD THROUGHOUT MY CAREER

I refuse to just take "yes" for an answer. I admit that I have a problem being overzealous and I sometimes go on and on in a kind of rapture about the ad campaign I've just presented to a client (which has already been enthusiastically accepted). I continue to make specific references to the ads and the TV spots strewn across the conference-room table, assuring my clients that the advertising will succeed, without conditions or qualifiers. ('No agency in today's advertising world promises success, because most agencies don't believe in the miracle of creativity.)

Yes, I plead guilty to over-selling, but when I finally walk out of the room, they believe in my work and, just as importantly, they believe in *me*.

41.
Open wide and say "aaah!"

If you're a creative in any business, think of yourself as a doctor giving a patient medicine that will save his life. I'm dead serious.

42.
To create great work, here's how you must spend your time:
1% Inspiration
9% Perspiration
90% Justification

I don't care how talented you are. If you're the kind of creative person who gets your best work produced — justifying and selling your work (to those around you, to your boss, to your client, to lawyers, to TV copy clearance, etc.) is what separates the sometimes good creative thinker from the consistently great one.

43.
Tell the Devil's Advocate in the room to go to Hell.

A self-appointed Devil's Advocate lurks in every meeting and, at the moment a decision is about to be finalized, says with a furrowed brow, "Let me be the Devil's Advocate." They always take the exact opposite and argue ad nauseam. That person is the instigator of group grope (see 25) and analysis paralysis (see 26) that smothers and suffocates any original idea, all in the name of careful, conservative thinking. Any creative idea is in danger with a Devil's Advocate in the room. Beware.

44.
When you're presenting a Big Idea, be prepared to answer dumb questions.

There's usually somebody in every meeting that just doesn't get it. Before the last word comes out of their lips, tear their doubts to shreds.

45.
But that doesn't mean you shouldn't (occasionally) kiss ass!

Copywriter Ron Holland worked with me on thousands of small space ads for Joe Baum and his dozen or more restaurants that were changing the face of Manhattan. Ron was a lonely bachelor and he was kind-of adopted by Joe and his wife, Ruth, who had him as a guest at their country home many weekends.
One Monday morning, as Ron and I were reviewing one of our campaigns with Joe, the symbiosis between Baum and Holland suddenly, inexplicably, turned explosive. They were at each other's throats cursing and screaming. I was aghast. Finally, Ron shouted at Baum **"Joe, I hope you die!"**
To which I quickly added, **"A rich man!"**
(Don't tell *me* I don't know how to kiss ass!)

46.
If all else fails, threaten to commit suicide.

At Doyle Dane Bernbach in 1959, I created a Passover subway poster for Goodman's Matzos. My headline was in Hebrew with two universally understood words (at least in New York), *Kosher for Passover*, and under it, a gigantic matzo. When the account man came back with a resounding no from the client, I went to my boss, Bill Bernbach, and insisted he make an appointment with Goodman's honcho, an Old Testament, bushy-eyebrowed tyrant, a master kvetch. The matzos maven yawned as I opened with a passionate pitch. When I unfurled my poster, he muttered, "I dun like it." I disregarded him and pressed forwards, selling my guts out. The tyrant tapped the desk for silence as one, then two, then three of his staff registered support for the powerful Hebrew headline. "No, no," he said, "I dun like it!" I had to make a final move – so I walked up to an open casement window. As I began to climb through the window, he shouted after me, "You going someplace?" He and his staff gasped at me as if I was some kind of meshuggener, poised on the outer ledge three floors above the pavement. I gripped the vertical window support with my left hand, waved the poster with my free hand, and screamed from the ledge at the top of my lungs,
"You make the matzo, I'll make the ads!"
"Stop, stop," said the old man, frantically. "Ve'll *run* it."
I climbed back into the room and thanked the patriarch for the nice way he received my work. As I was leaving, he shouted after me,
"Young man, if you ever qvit advertising, you got yourself ah job as ah matzos salesman!"

47.
A creative thinker is capable of looking at a business venture and creating a Big Idea that infinitely surpasses the vision of the CEO.

In 1982, Jiffy Lube, a pioneering quick oil-change company, came to my ad agency when they had five stores. We told them that if we could run a national TV campaign, they would be a 1,000 store national chain within three years. Arguing and begging, they finally gave us the okay to not only run a national TV campaign, but to control their marketing program. Overnight, we persuaded America to change their oil at Jiffy Lube, and in three years they had over *2,000 stations* nationwide!

48.
When you know a client is dead wrong about a marketing opportunity, create a brand name that blows his mind!

In the late 1970s, my agency acquired a new client, Stouffer's frozen foods. At our "nuptial" dinner with Stouffer's brass, I politely asked if they planned to go into *diet gourmet* frozen foods. They said diet foods were a back-burner item that required expensive ingredients, eeked out low profit margins, yada-yada. I pointed out that we were in the midst of an emerging health trend and more and more American women were working,

and it was incumbent on Stouffer's to develop a quality product in response to the zeitgeist. They dismissed my appeal. I couldn't sleep that night, chewed over their rejection of a diet gourmet line of frozen foods, and eureka!...***Lean Cuisine*** – a brand name that said everything that had to be said to describe a revolutionary product line. I sent the name pronto to the president of Stouffer's. For once, the concept needed no "selling" on my part: "Lean" said thin, "Cuisine" said delicious. The CEO ate it up, and a new and dynamic marketing category was born.

Sometimes all the "marketing" insight in the world can't move a client, but the creation of a truly great brand name can become a billion-dollar idea!

49.
It helps when you have a sharp-eyed client.

When asked to create a poster by Garry Kasparov's handlers
for the World Chess Championship between Kasparov
and his brilliant challenger, Anatoly Karpov, at the Hudson Theater
in Manhattan, I created the ultimate confrontation in
the fierce combat of chess. Kasparov's business managers
insisted that Kasparov, arguably the greatest chess
player in history, would be oblivious to it – and forbid me
to show it to him. But after an argument lost in
translation, I defied them, and when I presented the poster
to the Russian chess genius, the white chess piece
between his profile and Karpov's hit him like an emotional
illumination, and he gasped the words "*Na Zdorovye,
tovarich*! Kasparov and Karpov, nose to nose, and betveen them,
ah vite kveen!"

**Great work must be presented to the person that has
the power to accept your creations.** The problem is that the
underlings in any business or enterprise can always say
"No" (and many times do), but have no power to say "Yes" – so you
must get past them and **present to the decision-maker!**

GARRY KASPAROV VS. ANATOLY KARPOV 1990 WORLD CHESS CHAMPIONSHIP

OCTOBER 8 – NOVEMBER 10, 1990
NEW YORK CITY

50.
Research is the enemy of creativity – unless it's your own "creative" research (heh-heh).

Advertising is an art, not a science. If you create advertising to pass a research test (as almost all establishment agencies do), the "science" of advertising runs the show. Most of my ad campaigns would have flunked commercial pre-testing because edgy, sometimes mind-blowing concepts get ripped apart in group-grope "focus groups." I once used research (conceived and conducted by my agency) to create a gigantic marketing success for Quaker's Aunt Jemima pancake brand. Inexplicably, Quaker refused to market an Aunt Jemima *syrup*, a no-brainer if I ever poured one. Their management was adamant every time I brought it up. But I plunged ahead with a research questionnaire devised on Aunt Jemima pancake mix, including one question at the end of the survey asking consumers to name the syrup brand they used most recently – and I included the nonexistent Aunt Jemima syrup among a list of 10 brands. Eighty-nine out of 100 pancake eaters claimed they had purchased Aunt Jemima syrup that year! The honchos at Quaker were stunned and convinced by my results – and they finally plunged into the syrup business. Within a year, the new Aunt Jemima syrup became the best-selling syrup in America.
If you can't convince a client to produce a no-brainer win, manipulate them any way you can to win them over.

51.
When you present an entrepreneurial idea, if it takes more than three sentences to explain it to the money guys, it's not a Big Idea!

After three sentences of explanation, people's eyes glaze over.

52.
If you create truly great advertising, you can go far above and beyond the wildest expectations of your client!

When I told management at beleaguered ESPN (the 24-hour sports cable network) that I would cajole 15 superstar athletes, for zilch to perform in my *In Your Face* campaign, their president guffawed. In 1992, ESPN was perceived as a mickey-mouse sports network. To convince sports fans that ESPN was indeed dominant in TV sports, I went nose-to-nose with their president to let me produce an in-your-face campaign, showing him a list of 15 of America's hottest athletes of the day. "Lois, not one of them would cross the street for less than $50,000," he snarled.

But I cajoled every superstar on my hit list because I knew two things the honcho didn't know. ESPN had the possibility of becoming a giant and hadn't scratched the surface...and athletes loved appearing in my commercials.

The result of my campaign became a Harvard Business School case study on how to turn around a company's image. ESPN sold out all their advertising schedules and they went from worst to first in public opinion, rating ahead of ABC, CBS, and NBC. And they went on to implement my creative marketing plan that their obtuse president thought was a pipe dream on my part, including an ESPN magazine and ESPN sports bars. **If you must, drag your clients into a marketing breakthrough.**

"When the Moon comes out,
ESPN is *In Your Face!*"
WARREN MOON

53.
Never, ever, work for bad people.

On November 22, 1963, as soon as I got over the initial shock
after hearing John F. Kennedy had been shot, we called
all our clients to cancel their TV advertising. The president's
condition was still unclear and the networks hadn't
yet slapped a moratorium on advertising, but our clients agreed
this was no time for business as usual. But one of our
account men called J. Dan Brock, our National Airlines client,
who answered in his good ol' boy, southern drawl,
"I think you boys in New York are blowing this all out of proportion."
I jumped on the phone and said, "I'm sorry Dan, I guess
you haven't heard that the president's been *shot*!" "Sheeet, Lois,"
said Brock, "He's dead! Hell, we're *celebrating*!"
"Hey, Dan," I said in my Noo Yawk drawl, "Kiss my New York ass,"
slammed down the phone, and canceled all their
television commercials. The next morning (surprise, surprise)
J. Dan Brock fired us. Good riddance.
**When the news got around my agency as to why we were fired,
everybody could not have felt prouder.**
Don't ever, knowingly, work for bad people.

THE ASSASSINATION OF
JOHN F. KENNEDY
IN DALLAS, TEXAS, 1963

54.
Never eat shit.
(If it looks like shit,
and it smells like shit,
and it tastes like shit...
it's shit.)

If you're in a relationship (with your boss, supervisor, partner,
or client) and you suspect that you are continually
being used and/or abused, admit it—you're eating shit.
Without the courage to put an end to it,
you'll never create great work. Put an end to it.

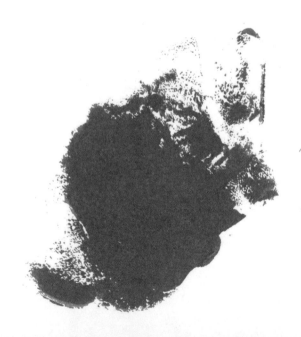

55.
To keep the Big Boys honest, speak Truth to Power.

Abraham Lincoln said, "To sin by silence
when they should protest makes cowards of men."
The best of us whose creations can be
thought of as art are cultural provocateurs,
infused with subversion against all
kinds of authority, even God.
Join those of us in the creative community
that are hard on big business moguls,
fat cats, "the authorities," courts,
politicians, Wall Street greed,
government that benefits
the wealthy at the expense of
the poor and powerless,
and anyone corrupted
by money and power.

Bob Dylan famously wrote
in his iconic indictment,
"Masters of War":
I think you will find
When your death takes its toll
All the money you made
Will never buy back your soul.

56.
Don't be a cry-baby!

A client could kill and kill and kill what you think is right for him
(the Abominable No-Man), but he can't *make* you run
bad work. You have the choice to fight back with better work, or find
better clients. Creative people in my field all cry over their
"great ads" that remain on tissue paper in their dark file drawers.
I say that you never *did* the job if you didn't sell it to
the client. The accurate measure of a human being is what he
or she actually gets done. In my life, I can't imagine any
taste worse than the taste of sour grapes. So, don't be a cry-baby.
Over the length of a bountiful creative career,
you must decide your own fate and what you produce.

Don't always expect praise from your client.

In 1964, I nagged a client, Joe Baum (who I worked with to create restaurants in New York), to take over a joint in Rockefeller Center called Holland House, where six old ladies ate salads every day at lunch. For two years, Joe kept telling me it was a lousy location. It was a block from the famous skating rink, and while it was a dark lonely street at night, I thought it would make a great Irish bar that would pack 'em in. "Lois," he kept insisting, "You do great advertising, but you don't know diddly about the restaurant business. **It's a lousy location!**" Finally, to get me off his back, Baum actually did take over the location, and in two months flat we opened Charley O's Bar & Grill & Bar. From the moment we opened, the place was a smash. I persuaded Bobby Kennedy, whose political advertising I was about to do, to announce at this new watering hole that he would run for the Senate. The TV coverage gave the impression that "famous Charley O's" had been around for 40 years! A little while later I was fishing for a compliment from my client. "Charley O's is a gold mine, ain't it Joe?" I said to Baum." "Of course, George," and with a straight face he said, **"it's a great location!"**

58.
If you think people are dumb, you'll spend a lifetime doing dumb work.

People are smart (a minority opinion in the boardrooms of most ad agencies). I've suffered being stuck with listening to other agency chairmen give talks, and I've been shocked and angered by the patronizing attitude of those agency biggies. Their recurring complaint is that people are stupid. Trust me, if you think people are dumb, you'll spend a lifetime doing dumb work. I think people are absolutely brilliant about advertising. They have a microchip in their heads that places a television commercial in its marketing context with lightning speed, enabling them to judge astutely. They "get" Big Ideas! Moreover, they always respond to an idea – a strong, central concept or image – especially if it is represented in a warm, human way. If you don't believe what I just said, you'll never do great work.

59.
"Too many notes, my dear Mozart, and too beautiful for our ears."

EMPEROR JOSEPH II

I've worked for plenty of tough clients. I relish working with benevolent tyrants – I usually get them to okay my work (not just my work, but my moxie!). I've made a few startling miscalculations – mistakenly assuming I would be working for an entrepreneurial personality with balls and passion. When I found out that I was completely wrong, and great work fell on the deaf ears of a bureaucrat, I (politely) walked. Big Ideas in any creative industry should be reserved for clients of vision and imagination – who can recognize talent and are determined to milk that talent to its limit.

Don't waste your time on the Emperor Josephs of the world.

60.
Woody Allen was right:
80% of life is showing up!

In 1962, my New York-based hot young ad agency caught the eye of the two top honchos of the Chicago-based Quaker Oats Company. They were in the midst of choosing a new ad agency, and even though they had a self-imposed rule of only hiring local agencies, they visited Papert Koenig Lois to size us up. They made no secret of the fact that they wanted to switch from their typical Establishment "marketing" agency to the ad agency that was triggering the Advertising Creative Revolution. Two days later, they both got on the telephone at 9.00 a.m. Chicago time (10.00 a.m. New York time) and painfully told us that they were in anguish with their decision, but felt they had to work with a local agency because of their need to call meetings at a moment's notice – and New York was a faraway land.

After hanging up the phone, my two partners and I looked at each other, our minds racing, and we blurted out to each other, "Let's race the hell to La Guardia Airport and be in their office before they get back from lunch!" We made it to La Guardia in half an hour, jumped on a plane (no security procedures in those days), 2 1/2 hours on a plane, then a fast cab ride, and breathlessly got to their office in the Merchandise Mart while they were still out to lunch! Half an hour later they walked into their waiting room, and you could have knocked them over with a feather when they saw us sprawled out on their comfy couches, thumbing through magazines. Thrilled and delighted at our gung-ho caper, they gave us their advertising account on the spot.

Think on your feet, make things happen, impress clients not only with your work, but with your hustle, desire, and chutzpah!

61.
I've been accused of being paranoid.
(You'd be paranoid too
if everyone were out to get you.)

I'll use every trick in the book to save my Big Ideas.
I've even threatened suicide (see 46). Sounds nuts.
I've always thought you were nuts if you went to a psychiatrist...
but you *weren't* nuts if you're paranoid! Having a healthy
paranoia helps protect a creative person's work, because, make
no mistake about it, they're all out to get you!
Living a life having your work being judged by the philistines
of the world is scary. They'll call you a flake.
They'll call you nuts.
Screw 'em.

62.
Any great creative idea should stun momentarily – it should *seem* to be outrageous.

Safe, conventional work is a ticket to oblivion.
Great creativity should stun, as modern art was
supposed to shock, by presenting the viewer
with an idea that seemingly suspends conventions of
understanding. In that swift interval between
the shock and the realization that what you are
presenting is not as outrageous
as it seems, you capture your audience.

63.
Sometimes, what the hell, go all out and be *totally* outrageous.

Sometimes I've gone (knowingly) overboard. In 1985, a young fashion designer with a boyish grin and an unpronounceable name was totally unknown when he was launched with a Tommy Hilfiger store on Manhattan's Upper West Side. The first ad in my campaign (and an identical outdoor billboard blatantly placed across the street from the offices of the schmatta kings) challenged the reader with an outrageous, audacious claim. Overnight, the burning question in town became **"Who the hell is T____ H_____?"** Tommy Hilfiger became instantly famous and set off an avalanche of national publicity within days. This original Tommy campaign was a self-fulfilling prophecy because the young Hilfiger soon became the most famous and successful designer brand in the world.

P.S. The Hilfiger ad infuriated the fashion industry. In *Newsweek* and *People* magazine, Calvin Klein insisted we had spent $20,000,000 (two zeros too many). A few months after the ad appeared, Mr. Klein, obviously livid as he watched Tommy's growing fame, saw me having dinner with my wife and friends one night at Mr. Chow's, strode over, stuck his finger in my face, and blurted out: "Do you know it took me twenty years to get where Hilfiger is today!" I politely grabbed his finger, bent it, and answered: **"Schmuck! Why take twenty years when you can do it in twenty days?!"**

THE 4 GREAT AMERICAN DESIGNERS
FOR MEN ARE:

R_____L_____
P____E_____
C_____K_____
T___H_____

THIS IS THE
LOGO OF THE
LEAST KNOWN OF
THE FOUR

282 Columbus Avenue
at 73rd Street
New York, New York 10023
(212) 877-1270

BILLBOARD FOR TOMMY HILFIGER,
TIMES SQUARE, NEW YORK, 1985

64.
A truly great ad campaign is driven by a Big Idea that contains:
1. A memorable slogan!
2. A memorable visual!

A memorable visual, synergistically blending with memorable words that create imagery which communicates in a nanosecond, immediately results in an intellectual and human response. The word imagery is too often associated purely with visuals, but it is much more than that: imagery is the conversion of an idea into a theatrical cameo, an indelible symbol, a scene that becomes popular folklore, an iconographic image. And this imagery should be expressed in words and visuals or, ideally, both! Shown is a sissy, superstar tour de force of some of the greatest macho sports icons of the 1960s, weeping and moaning *I want my Maypo!* (an oatmeal cereal) on TV, a single-minded merger of words and pictures that American kids ate up.

MICKEY MANTLE   **WILLIE MAYS**

"I want my Maypo!"

DON MEREDITH

JOHNNY UNITAS

OSCAR ROBERTSON

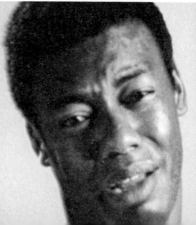

65.
To constantly inspire breakthrough conceptual thinking, I go to the Metropolitan Museum of Art, religiously, every Sunday.

Lou Dorfsman, design chief for CBS Radio and later the CBS Television Network for over 40 years, once said, "In reality, creativity is the ability to reach inside yourself and drag forth from your very soul an idea." However, nothing comes from nothing. You must continuously feed the inner beast that sparks and inspires. I contend the DNA of talent is stored within the great museums of the world. Museums are custodians of epiphanies and these epiphanies enter the central nervous system and the deep recesses of the mind. The shock of an epiphany, a word derived from the Greek *epiphanie*, has been an almost daily occurrence since I was a youngster, mystically echoing throughout much of my work. For example, I transformed the Met's excruciating image by Francesco Botticini of Saint Sebastian into a 1967 *Esquire* cover depicting Muhammad Ali (see 76).

My spiritual day of worship is spent each Sunday at New York's Metropolitan Museum of Art, where I experience, without fail, the shock of the old. (In London, go to the British Museum; in France, visit the Louvre; in Madrid, the Prado; you get the idea.) **Mysteriously, the history of the art of mankind can inspire breakthrough conceptual thinking, in any field.**

66.

"The things that you're liable To read in the Bible – It ain't necessarily so."

IRA GERSHWIN, AMERICAN LYRICIST

No, the world was not created in six days.

No, dinosaurs and people never coexisted.

No, a teenager won't go blind if he masturbates too often.

No, Clifford Irving never met Howard Hughes.

No, there were no Weapons of Mass Destruction in Iraq.

No, most "health foods" ain't.

No, *Mad Men* is not an accurate depiction of advertising in the 1960s.

No, Barack Obama is not an "illegal" president.

No, Denial ain't just a river in Egypt.

You can't live your life as a skeptic...but be skeptical.
More than ever, in this age of internet technology,
misinformation comes at us second by second, in a tidal wave.
**A thinking person must read, study, question,
evaluate, and not let the bullshitters bullshit you.**

ADAM AND EVE
PETER PAUL RUBENS, 1597

67.

Crave immortality!

The film star James Dean was right when he said,
"The only greatness is immortality" (defined only by a body
of creativity you leave behind when you're dead).

68.
Picasso was right when he said, "Art is the lie that tells the truth."

Picasso's definition is wonderfully relevant to advertising in today's marketing-wise world, where almost all products are comparable in quality. When advertising is great advertising—when it's inventive, irreverent, audacious—it literally becomes a benefit of the product, and Picasso's "lie" becomes the truth. Cars drive better. Food tastes better. Perfume smells better. If you find it hard to agree with this basic belief, you may find it extremely difficult to understand the magic of advertising.

Food tastes better!

Perfume smells better!

Cars drive better!

69.
Maybe the best way to define your future is to reinvent it.

In tough economic times, look for unique ways to ignite your career. For instance, designing movie titles was once a thrilling creative challenge. Saul Bass (1920 – 99) invented the art of creating movie titles that literally branded movies with conceptual, animated graphic power (*Anatomy of a Murder*, *The Man with the Golden Arm*, *Vertigo*, *North by Northwest*, and *Psycho*). With hundreds of independent films being produced as we speak, there are endless opportunities to help visionary directors start off their films, and your career, with a bang!

In today's ever-changing business landscape, web-site design, app design, computer animation, video-game programming – a whole new world of unforseen opportunities – are on the way.
If your job search is getting you nowhere, reinvent your future.

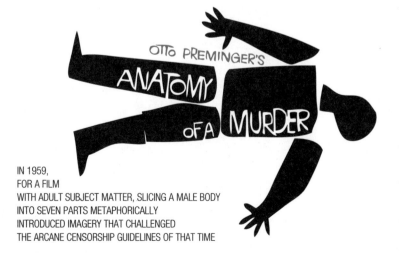

IN 1959,
FOR A FILM
WITH ADULT SUBJECT MATTER, SLICING A MALE BODY
INTO SEVEN PARTS METAPHORICALLY
INTRODUCED IMAGERY THAT CHALLENGED
THE ARCANE CENSORSHIP GUIDELINES OF THAT TIME

70.
Most great slogans have the brand name *in the slogan* (even twice!).

When you're creating a slogan that powerfully nails a product's unique selling proposition, try to include the product name! In 1989, *Make time for Time* was my four-word slogan with the product name used *twice*! The mnemonic slogan asked for the sale, and acknowledged how busy we all were, strongly suggesting that busy readers carve out some quality time for *Time*.

People
who have
too much
to read

MAKE
TIME
FOR
TIME

My favorite slogans by other creatives that include the brand name:

Avis is only No.2.

With a name like Smucker's, it has to be good.

The Independent. It is. Are you?

Isn't that Raquel Welch behind those Foster Grants?

Have an Amsterdam good time.

I ♥ New York.

Schweppervescence.

Raise your hand if you're Sure.

Absolut Perfection.

If you thought the 1980's was the decade of the Information Revolution, wait till you see the 90s! You're going to have news coming at you from all angles—tv, radio, newspapers, magazines, fax machines, computers. To stay ahead, you can try to read and absorb more than humanly possible. Or, cut through it all – carve out some quality time and make time for TIME. For readers and advertisers alike, it's time well spent.

71.

When the mayor of New York exceeded his reelection war chest, he begged me to help get the big boys to pay his campaign debts. I hadda be creative. I got it – I'll make Koch *beg* for it!

Even the flamboyant Ed Koch didn't have the hubris to flat out ask the big money boys to pay his enormous campaign debts without some kind of explanation. So I designed an invitation for a Gala Fundraising Roast to raise the bucks. The invite was a small accordion folder that showed just the head and shoulders of a benign Mayor Koch, but when you opened the accordion, you saw the whole picture of a pleading mayor in trouble, with both hands holding his completely empty pockets, sticking out from his pants. In one bold stroke, the mayor fessed up and charmed the New York power elite. The folder became the talk of the town and drew a huge response, packing the vast banquet room in the Sheraton Centre with fat-cats in tuxedos. To greet them as they entered, I placed a life-size cutout blow-up of Hizzoner, displaying his empty pockets. New York's movers and shakers actually emptied their pockets and strutted around all evening imitating the mayor! The money was raised, the slate was wiped clean, and even his worst enemies admired his Big Apple chutzpah.

Be creative – there are lots of ways to skin a (fat) cat.

Gala
Fundraising Roast for
Mayor Edward I. Koch

Roast:

Hon. Walter F. Mondale
Hon. William H. Mulligan

Rebuttal:

Ed Koch

Finance Committee
Chairman

Peter J. Solomon

Dinner Co-Chairs

Sol C. Chaikin
William M. Ellinghaus
Harold L. Fisher
Bess Myerson
Vitto J. Pitta
John Torres
Lloyd A. Williams

Tuesday
September 15
Sheraton Centre

Cocktails at 7:00 pm
Dinner at 8:00 pm

Dinner Co-ordinator

Ellin Delsener

72.
Twenty lovely ladies carrying my $10 picket signs stopped the most powerful politician in New York history.

In 1962, New York's Highway Commissioner Robert Moses, the master-broker who constructed highways in, out, over, under, and through New York with little concern for mass transit needs, decreed that a four-lane highway was needed to carry cars across the 32-mile (50-km) length of Fire Island.

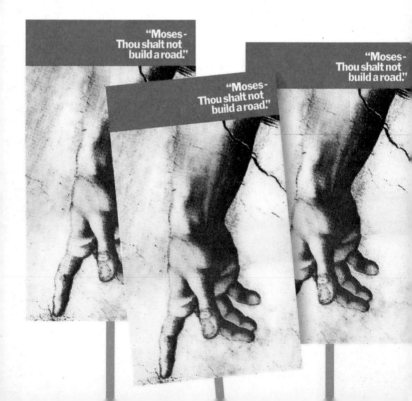

Plans were drawn to construct the highway right through the skinny line of summer homes on Fire Island. It would turn an idyllic community into a California freeway. My family had recently discovered this perfect summer place to raise two young boys, and my wife Rosie got mad as hell and organized the Tenants Committee to Save Fire Island to prevent the Moses road. To help her win the battle, I did a poster – my 11th commandment for Moses! I wanted our neighbors and the powers that be to understand that God had more authority than Moses. I produced dozens of large posters as picket signs for Rosie and her committee.

And boy, did they picket! Armed with the might of the hand of an accusing God, Rosie's housewives told Moses at a public hearing where to get off! The road was never built.

Once again, and for almost no money, creativity can solve any problem!

"Moses- Thou shalt not build a road."

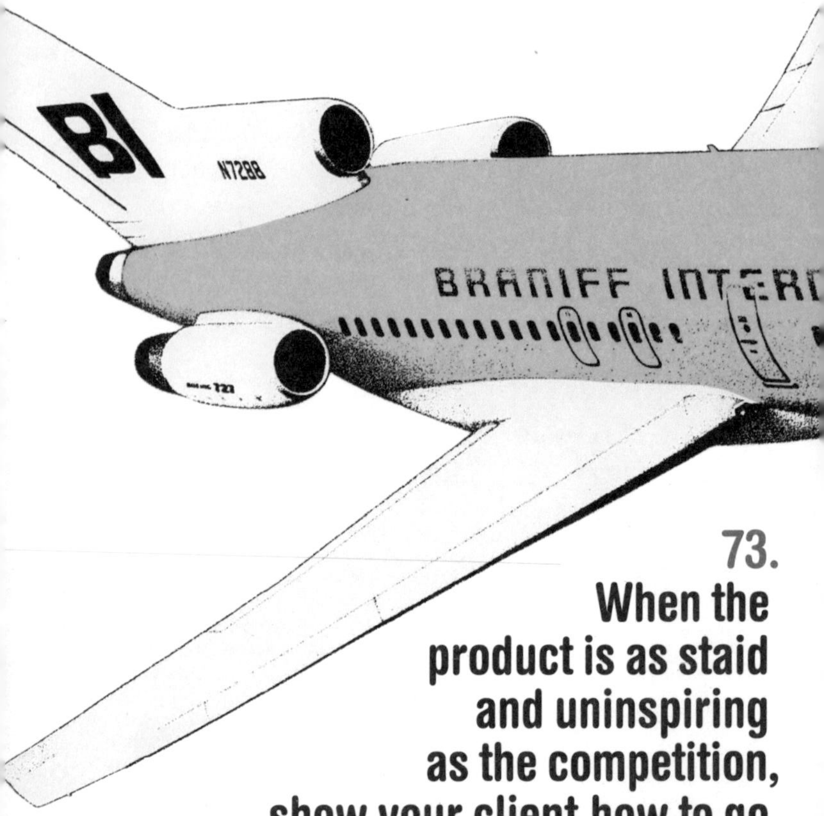

73.
When the
product is as staid
and uninspiring
as the competition,
show your client how to go
above and beyond.

In the mid-1960s, Wonder Woman Mary Wells, talented, tough, and good looking, moved from Doyle Dane Bernbach to Jack Tinker & Partners, and lassoed the gun-slinging Texan, Harding Lawrence, as a client *and* a husband. Lawrence had recently been installed at Braniff International as their honcho and he knew the airline was as lackluster as his main competitor, American Airlines.

With the Braniff account in hand, the go-getter Mary Wells Lawrence, knowing her newlywed was committed to action, outlined a daring program that would have boggled the mind of an ordinary client. Leaving Tinker, she founded Wells, Rich, Greene and envisioned a spanking new Braniff: Emilio Pucci designed "Space Age" uniforms worn by beauty contest-winning "hostesses"; Alexander Girard designed plane interiors with 57 variations of Herman Miller's fabrics; there were plush *real* leather seats; elegantly served gourmet cuisine; vibrant new terminals; and...the pièce de résistance, painting the exterior of the complete Braniff fleet, from nose to tail, in nine glorious colors – all advertised to the public with the slogan, **The End of the Plain Plane.** Harding Lawrence did it all, feverishly, and transformed Braniff into the chicest (and suddenly successful) airline in the world. Now *that's* a marriage made in heaven.

$ellebrity: Learn the art of using celebrities to sell a product.

Enlisting a celebrity to sell cat food, an airline, off-track betting, an analgesic, or a lube job would seem to be a delusionary strategy, fraught with irrationality (and seeming suspiciously to be motivated by a starfucker mentality). But let's face it, it's a starstruck world. We're all suckers for a famous face. A celebrity can add almost instant style, atmosphere, feeling, and/or meaning to any place, product, or situation – unlike any other advertising "symbol." The trick is to conceptually choose celebs that will ignite your advertising concept (and then convince them to forgo big buck compensation!). Enlist the perfect celebrity that gives you the power to project new language and startling imagery that enters the popular culture, and advertising communication takes on a dimension that leaves competitive products in the dust.

When celebrity...is transformed into $ellebrity.

ANNOUNCED IN PRINT ADS, GIVEN EACH MONTH TO A POWERHOUSE CELEBRITY (FOR A FEE TO THEIR FAVORITE CHARITY), WOMEN WHO WOULDN'T BE CAUGHT DEAD IN A PANTYHOSE AD LINED UP TO RECEIVE AN AWARD FROM NO NONSENSE, A FUNCTIONAL, UTILITARIAN LEGWEAR THAT SEEMINGLY HAD *ZERO* SEX APPEAL: FAYE DUNAWAY, GOVERNOR ANN RICHARDS, GLORIA STEINEM, BARBARA STREISAND, TINA TURNER, OPRAH WINFREY, AND 35 OTHERS GAVE NO NONSENSE *IMMEDIATE* SEX APPEAL

THE NO NONSENSE
AMERICAN WOMAN AWARD
TO ELIZABETH TAYLOR

AFTER A LIFETIME OF
PASSION AND COMPASSION,
SHE REMAINS ONE OF
THE MOST BEAUTIFUL AND INSPIRING
ROLE MODELS IN THE WORLD –
THANKS IN NO SMALL PART TO HER
PIONEERING CAMPAIGN
AGAINST AIDS

75.
What a difference a name makes!

If the name of a revolutionary product is weak and unambitious, create a great one (along with an eye-popping ad campaign). In late 2010, I was approached by the inventor of custom-made, adjustable-focus, prescription eyeglasses that allow the wearer to move a tiny slider on the bridge, where you can focus on the page of a book, a computer screen, a movie, or a distant mountain – miraculously restoring the sight of your youth. Dr. Stephen Kurtin and his marketing team had named them Trufocals, and he wanted me to create an ad campaign. I told him, point blank, that after hearing what a phenomenal product it was, Trufocals was a weak, hard to remember, unambitious name.

To do the advertising, I insisted on changing the brand name, an expensive proposition since they were already advertising in some areas of the U.S. Three days later I presented the name Superfocus, with an in-your-face logotype and a slogan, *See the world, far and near, in Superfocus*, along with an ad campaign of five celebrity users, whose punchline in TV spots was *Now I see the world...In Superfocus!* The power of the Superfocus name and the TV campaign, running on national cable TV, instantly made these brilliantly engineered glasses (used by NASA astronauts on the Space Shuttle and International Space Station) an out-of-this-world marketing success!

Remember, you know more about branding than your client.
(That's why they hired you!)

SUPERFOCUS™

SEE THE WORLD, FAR AND NEAR, IN SUPERFOCUS!

"Whenever
I hear those iconic words
'O say can you see'
I always say to myself,
'*Not that good!*'
Bifocals, trifocals, progressives,
nothing had clarity.
But now I see the world...
in *Superfocus*!
And that's no bullshit!"

PENN JILLETTE,
AMERICAN COMEDIAN
AND ILLUSIONIST

76.

In an age when heroes are villainized and villains are lionized, a creative image can make an iconic statement.

In 1967, when Muhammad Ali refused induction into the army, he was widely condemned as a draft-dodger, and even a traitor. When he had converted to Islam, he had become a black Muslim minister, and Ali refused military service as a conscientious objector because of his new religious views. A federal jury sentenced him to five years in jail for draft evasion, and boxing commissions then stripped him of his title and denied him the right to fight, in the prime of his fighting years. This incredibly controversial *Esquire* cover became an instant iconic symbol of a period of nonviolent protest in those turbulent times. My statement nailed down the plight of many Americans who took a principled stand against the Vietnam War. Three years after I depicted Ali as the martyr Saint Sebastian, the U.S. Supreme Court unanimously threw out Ali's conviction.

No matter what stage you are in your career, use your creativity to stand up for our heroes, and protect your culture against the villains.

APRIL 1968
PRICE $1

Esquire

THE MAGAZINE FOR MEN

EVERLAST

The Passion of Muhammad Ali

"THE MOST ICONIC IMAGE OF THE 1960s WAS GEORGE LOIS' *ESQUIRE* COVER DEPICTING ALI AS SAINT SEBASTIAN, TYING TOGETHER THE INCENDIARY ISSUES OF THE VIETNAM WAR, RACE, AND RELIGION. THE IMAGE IS SO POWERFUL THAT SOME PEOPLE REMEMBER WHERE THEY WERE WHEN THEY SAW IT FOR THE FIRST TIME."

77.

"The secret of all effective advertising is not the creation of new and tricky words and pictures, but one of putting familiar words and pictures into new relationships."

LEO BURNETT, LEGENDARY ADMAN

In the 1960s, in *Life* magazine, I put an end to ubiquitous penthouses and smiling couples in deadly-dull booze ads, and shocked and delighted vodka drinkers, and the ad world, by showing an amorous Wolfschmidt bottle hitting on a tomato (in my day, slang for a hot babe). A week later, romancing an orange, the phallic bottle gets hit with the comeback, "Who was that tomato I saw you with last week?" Week after week, Wolfschmidt bantered with lemons, limes, olives, and onions, all in sexy double entendre. Familiar words and pictures put into startling new (erotic) relationships! **The secret of creativity? Make it new!**

"You sweet doll, I appreciate you.
I've got taste.
I'll bring out the real orange in you.
I'll make you famous.
Kiss me."

"Who was that tomato
I saw you with last week?"

78.
I was never a fan of the David Ogilvy School of Advertising (but this ad was an eye-opener).

Read David Ogilvy's stifling rules and regulations on art direction in his highly regarded book, *Confessions of an Advertising Man*, to understand how far apart he and I were on the subject of creativity. **My credo is that the only rule in advertising – is that there are no rules!** But what I think the Ogilvy culture certainly understood, and practiced, was the need to create a specific, memorable, and unique visual identification that drew you into their long, but beautifully crafted, body copy. The Ogilvy masterpiece was *The man in the Hathaway Shirt*, stiffly but elegantly posing, ad after ad, wearing an overly crisp Hathaway shirt, and an eye-popping, aristocratic eye patch, and ordained with the name Baron Wrangell (some sort of English wit, I gathered).

P.S. In 1959, before I started my own ad agency in 1960, Mr. Ogilvy actually tried to convince me to go to Ogilvy & Mather as their head art director, but I knew his rules were not for me. He was one of the first people to call and congratulate me when I founded Papert Koenig Lois.

Hathaway and the Duke's stud groom

IT ALL STARTED with Richard Tattersall, the Duke of Kingston's stud groom. He dressed his horses in magnificent check blankets. Then English tailors started using Mr. Tattersall's checks for gentlemen's waistcoats.

Now Hathaway takes the Tattersall one step further. With the help of an old Connecticut mill, we have scaled down this classic pattern to miniature proportions, so that you can wear it in New York. Yet its implication of landed gentry still remains.

You can get this Hathaway miniature Tattersall in red and grey (as illustrated), navy and blue, or mahogany and beige. Between board meetings you can amuse yourself counting the various hallmarks of a Hathaway shirt: 22 single-needle stiches to the inch, big buttons, square-cut cuffs. And so forth.

The price is $8.95. For the name of your nearest store, write C.F. Hathaway, Waterville, Maine. In New York, call OXford 7-5566.

79.
Most designers forget that their work must talk to human beings.

The majority of logos and packaging are abstract, or obscure or unclear, or puzzling or geometric, or all of these things. Most of all, they're uncommunicative. A design of any kind must say something about the product to its customer. It must contain an essential idea. It must convey at a glance your feelings about *yourself* and it must communicate the raison d'etre of the *product*. It must communicate personality, it must have blood running through it, it must have a twinkle in its eye, it must have a grin on its mush. It must have a quickly recognizable *face*. A solid marketing idea must be the bone structure of that face. The design explains that idea. **If you can't get meaning into your design, there's no meaning to your work.** (And if you're an entrepreneur founding a new company or product, get thee to a talented designer!)

LOGOS BY
GEORGE LOIS,
1962–2011

INDONESIAN TOBACCO CO.

THE HANGAR

80.
All your ad campaigns must be built-in PR campaigns!

Many of my ad campaigns became overnight PR sensations.
For instance, in 1967 I created the first TV campaign for
a Wall Street brokerage firm, the totally unknown Edwards & Hanly.
The legendary TV talk-show host Johnny Carson, from
The Tonight Show, loved the spots (they only ran in the New York area)
and mimicked the punchlines nightly. But the rest of the nation
didn't "get it." So he had to show the spots on his *national* broadcast,
so America could understand his references. In a 10-second spot,
the boxer Joe Louis, who had unfairly lost all his money to Uncle Sam,
looked into the camera and said, "Edwards & Hanly, where were
you when I needed you?" Carson mimicked the line almost nightly.
In another spot, Mickey Mantle, in his down-home twang, said,
"Boy I'm telling you when I came up to the big leagues, I was a shufflin,'
grinnin,' head-duckin,' country boy. Well I'm still a country boy,
but I know a man down at Edwards & Hanly. I'm learnin,' I'm learnin."
Carson said, *I'm learning, I'm learning* to his guests over a dozen
times in a few months. In yet another spot a kid says, "My daddy's an
astronaut!" A second kid says, "My daddy's a fireman!" A third
kid says, "*My* daddy works for Edwards & Hanly!" Then you hear the
first two kids' voiceover say, "Wowwww!" *Wowwww!* became
another Carson punchline. Three months after the campaign started,
Edwards & Hanly had opened thousands of new accounts
and became the third best-known investment broker in America.
**If your advertising doesn't have the power to become
a topic of conversation for everyone in the nation, you forfeit
the chance for it to be famous.**

"I'm learning."
I'm learning.

81.
If you're going to criticize something, don't hold back.

Marc Connelly (1890–1980), the American playwright and author of *The Green Pastures*, was being treated like a country bumpkin at a posh New York restaurant by drama critics Robert Benchley and John McLain. Connelly, miffed, rejected a bottle of a particularly abominable wine they had ordered by smartly telling the sommelier, **"Break the bottle, smash the barrel, and uproot the vineyard!"** The great playwright related the story to me, then whispered "I showed those city-slickers how to reject a bottle of wine!" **Don't be kind when you're judging work.** It doesn't help to give a soothing criticism to co-workers or to those who work for you when they show you bad work. When they finally succeed, they'll thank you for the honest critiques (maybe).

82.
Speak up, goddamit!

If you've got something to say, if you have a real idea,
if you're burning inside to get something out,
to get something done, to criticize what's going on,
stand up and speak out! Live, and work,
as truthfully, and creatively, and as outspokenly as you can.
(But if you're afraid to speak out, maybe it's
because it's just not worth saying.)

83.
Present your ideas without saying "y'know," "like," and "umm" every other sentence.

Umm, I mean, y'know, like I said, if you wrote the way
millions of people talk these days, you'd be considered a
dummy—like, umm, know what I mean? Okay?

84.
Sometimes the shocking way to solve a forbidding problem is to simply tell the truth.

In 1959, *Think Small* was the Big Idea that sold a Nazi car in a Jewish town in a New York nanosecond. Before Julian Koenig wrote the ad, all car ads were pure fantasy, using flattering illustrations or heavily retouched photographs to lengthen the lines of the brand being advertised. And the glitzy, glamorous imagery was accompanied by glib and meaningless copy claims. The bigger the vehicle, the better. Only a weird American would purchase such a small, ugly car, and, ouch, it was common knowledge that before WW II, Der Führer himself had given Dr. Ferdinand Porsche the order to invent "The People's Car." But when *Think Small* launched the Volkswagen campaign, their sales never looked back. America loved the ads – and it learned to love the car. Koenig's copy simply told the truth about a small car that got great gas mileage, and art director Helmut Krone showed a tiny "beetle" in lackluster black and white, with a simplicity that proved far more powerful and persuasive than flash and empty flights of fancy. The Doyle Dane Bernbach campaign ran for years with a creative strategy so solid any number of talented DDB writers were able to continue creating brilliant ads for years – the car ran out of gas before the campaign did.
Sometimes the Big Idea is hiding in the truth.

P.S. Six months later, I convinced Koenig to join me in leaving DDB to start Papert Koenig Lois, destined to be the second creative agency in the world.

Think small.

Ten years ago, the first Volkswagens were imported into the United States.

These strange little cars with their beetle shapes were almost unknown.

All they had to recommend them were 32 miles to the gallon (regular gas, regular driving), an aluminum air-cooled rear engine that would go 70 mph all day without strain, sensible size for a family and a sensible price-tag too.

Beetles multiply; so do Volkswagens. In 1954, VW was the best-selling import car in America. It has held that rank each year since in 1959, over 150,000 Volkswagens were sold, including 30,000 station wagons and trucks.

Volkswagen's snub-nose is now familiar in fifty states of the Union: as American as apple strudel. In fact, your VW may well be made with Pittsburgh steel stamped out on Chicago presses (even the power for the Volkswagen plant is supplied by coal from the U.S.A.).

As any VW owner will tell you, Volkswagen service is excellent and it is everywhere. Parts are plentiful, prices low. (A new fender, for example, is only $21.75.) No small factor in Volkswagen's success.

Today, in the U.S.A. and 119 other countries, Volkswagens are sold faster than they can be made. Volkswagen has become the world's fifth largest automotive manufacturer by thinking small. More and more people are thinking the same.

85.

I was convinced the conviction of Rubin "Hurricane" Carter, sentenced to 300 years in jail for allegedly killing three white people in a New Jersey bar, was an outrageous racial injustice. I had to do something to get him out of the slammer – I got it! I'm an adman, I'll run a tiny ad in *The New York Times* on page 2!

This ad was the opening salvo in waging a guerrilla war to free the innocent Hurricane. I visited Rubin Carter in Trenton State Prison to tell him what I was planning. A few days later I ran it in the news section of the national edition of *The New York Times*, the most influential paper in America. Within a week I enlisted 82 distinguished citizens, including Hank Aaron, Dave Anderson, Harry Belafonte, Jimmy Breslin, Ellen Burstyn, Dyan Cannon, Johnny Cash, Pete Hamill, Rev. Jesse Jackson, Ed Koch, Norman Mailer, Arthur Penn, George Plimpton, Burt Reynolds, Al Ruddy, Gay Talese, Bill Walton, and Bud Yorkin, with Muhammad Ali as the chairman. The ad kept millions of people in America from swallowing their toast that morning as they were reading *The Times*. **It's amazing what we creative communicators can accomplish– like helping spring an innocent man by running a tiny ad!**

Counting today, I have sat in prison 3,135 days for a crime I did not commit.

If I don't get a re-trial, I have 289 years to go. Six months ago the 'eyewitnesses' who testified they saw me leaving a bar in which 3 people had been killed, admit they gave false testimony. Despite this, the judge who sentenced me won't give me a re-trial. Why?

**RUBIN HURRICANE CARTER
NO. 45472
TRENTON STATE PRISON**

86.
Keep up the fight against racism, no matter what the cost.

In 1975, after enlisting Muhammad Ali to lead the fight to free
Rubin "Hurricane" Carter, who was framed by police and
prosecutors in Paterson, New Jersey (see 85), *The Hurricane Fund*
organized Hurricane Benefits all over Manhattan to continue
our fight for a new trial. The press ran hundreds of major stories,
culminating when Ali led a march of 10,000 protesters
past Trenton State Prison, where Carter had been incarcerated for
over 10 years. The Hurricane cause was sweeping
the nation. In the midst of the torrent of publicity, I was called into
the office of the president of Cutty Sark scotch whisky,
a $5 million client at my ad agency. I walked into Ed Horrigan's
office, and without a hello, he barked, "Lois, stop working
for the nigger or I'll fire you." I didn't blink. I told him I believed
in Carter's innocence and would not turn my back on him.
Horrigan, red-faced, stomped to the door of his sprawling office,
opened it, and gave me an ultimatum: "Last chance, Lois,
yes or no! Give me a one-word answer." I said, "No." The next day
he gave my agency the gate. I've always been proud
of doing the right thing. My advice to everyone reading this book:
**Do the right thing so you can be proud of yourself,
till the day you die.**

MUHAMMAD ALI LEADING A PROTEST MARCH
TO THE NEW JERSEY STATE CAPITOL
(BEHIND HIM IS GEORGE LOIS WITH HIS WIFE ROSIE)

87.

"What if we can get Bob Dylan to write a protest song and then perform a concert at Madison Square Garden?!"

Sometimes "what if" can become a reality. Admittedly, a great deal of wishful thinking comes into play, but conjuring outlandish "what if's" and making them come to life...that's creativity. In 1975, after years as a recluse, Bob Dylan went back to his roots, hitting the road with his Rolling Thunder Revue. In the midst of his whirlwind tour, my Rubin Carter Defense Committee was raising hell publicizing the story of how the outspoken fighter had been framed (see 85). A call here, some begging there, and I got backstage at a gig in Connecticut to go eye-to-eye with the passionate poet who I instinctively felt would be in total sympathy with Muhammad Ali and me in an attempt to right a brutal racial injustice. You're looking at a photo of me and Paul Sapounakis (my co-organizer) doing a Svengali on Dylan, convincing him of Carter's innocence and goading him to write a song and "maybe even, er, well, maybe even a concert, Bob?" A few weeks later he composed *Hurricane*, protesting Carter's conviction, and performed it to tremendous emotional response from his young audiences, and (gasp!) performed it in not one, but two *Night of the Hurricane* concerts – the first, inexplicably, in *prison*, then a few days later, a smashing performance in Madison Square Garden.

"What if" is the seed of breathtaking creative ideas.

In 1988, the United States Supreme Court ruled that Carter had been unjustly convicted, and in 1990, after 22 years, Rubin Carter was a free man.

BOB DYLAN CONCERT,
MADISON SQUARE GARDEN,
DECEMBER 8, 1975

Dear Gael Greene,

After all those wonderful meals we've had together.

Restaurant Associates

NEW YORK MAGAZINE, OCTOBER 5, 1970

88.
Deflate a catastrophic review...
with gentle (?) humor.

Gael Greene, *New York* magazine's restaurant critic, wrote a withering
review in 1970 of Restaurant Associates, the most inspired
and creative chain of gourmet restaurants in America. She was
especially rough on The Four Seasons, probably the finest
restaurant experience in New York, then and now. I thought she was
overly and unfairly critical, but the dirty deed was done.
Her article sent shock waves through Restaurant Associates and
business fell off ominously, with their stock taking a beating
on the American Stock Exchange. RA went panicky, then became
furious. They told me to cancel all their ads in *New York*
magazine. I got them to calm down and instead of allowing them
to vent their rage in a self-destructive way, I convinced
them to run an ad (in the very magazine that bombed them!).
My "Dear Gael Greene" missive, in sweet but no uncertain
terms, clearly said to savvy readers, "We fed Gael Greene's face
dozens of times – and now she bites the hand that feeds her?"
Fans of Restaurant Associates cheered when they saw this "rejoinder"
in the very next issue of *New York* – the stock rebounded and
soared, and the reservations mounted.
(A few weeks later, I invited a disarmed Gael Greene to lunch –
at The Four Seasons, natch.)

**The lesson? Fight back, not with bare knuckles,
but with a velvet glove.**

The talented art director's responsibility is to produce:

Great advertising created with a *great* copywriter!

"Some of my favorite performers are horses."

NyBets OTB

Wheeee, Pirelli!

Sure you can put Pirelli fantastico steel-belted radial tires on your car. Pirelli has tires that fit almost all American and imported cars. Capish?

PIRELLI

Great advertising created with a *fair* copywriter!

Great
advertising
created
with
a *lousy*
copywriter!

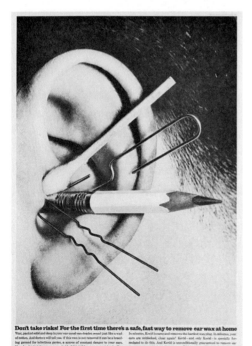

Great
advertising
created
without a
copywriter!

In a team that
produces advertising
in an ad agency,
the ultimate decision
must be in
the hands of the
art director.

90.
A creative person without a sense of humor has a serious problem.

A physicist, doctor, accountant, lawyer, garbage collector, etc. without a sense of humor can still be terrific at what they do. But a creative person who is humorless could never produce consistently great work in communicating with warmth and humanity to the vast majority of the populace. Humor in creativity is like humor in life. People often ask me, "Does humor work in advertising?" but that's a stupid question. Does anyone ever ask, "Does humor work in *life*?" If humor is appropriate and funny (if it ain't funny, we ain't talking humor), it should "work." The question should be, "How can you possibly create *without* humor?" Certainly, in all forms of communication, humor is a natural way to win someone's heart. In examining my work, lectures, and books I have written over the years, it's difficult to isolate "humor" as a category because it runs through almost everything I do – and through most of my waking hours. Humor disarms and makes one more accepting of thoughts and images that could be hard to take in serious discourse. Say something serious in a funny way, and you can win over people every time.
Wit wakes up the mind. We're talking serious comedy here!

IF YOU DON'T THINK THE ADS ON
THE FACING PAGE ARE FUNNY,
YOU DON'T HAVE A SENSE OF HUMOR

WE'RE PUSHING LEOTARDS

Cold and getting colder: now's the time to push stretch tights. Here's how Chemstrand helps you do it. With a full-page color supplement (theme: Tights for every use and age) that Chemstrand Publicity just released to newspapers in 100 key markets. With a special Promotion Kit containing two counter cards that are corkers, and a host of selling tips. (Look for the kit around December 1.) Tie in your windows, ads, interior displays. There's big business in leotards. Get your hands on some.

Chemstrand nylon

A Coty Cremestick turned Alice Pearce…into Joey Heatherton.

91.
"When you got it – flaunt it!"

When you got it – flaunt it! is a colloquialism that is a standard entry
in anthologies of American sayings. It was created in 1967 as
a theme for memorable Braniff airlines advertising – a zany, outrageous
campaign that featured some of the world's oddest couples,
exchanging the screwiest and most sophisticated chatter heard on TV.
I paired Pop Art guru Andy Warhol with a clueless Sonny Liston...
Yankee pitching great Whitey Ford with the surreal Salvador Dali...

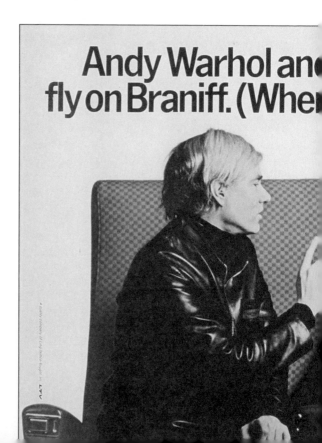

the British comedienne Hermione Gingold with Hollywood tough-guy George Raft...and the poet Marianne Moore with crime writer, Mickey Spillane. Predictably perhaps, *When you got it – flaunt it!* became synonymous with my career, and is now used in American popular culture to recognize any hip, outspoken personality. So, to all you aspiring, outspoken creative talents, my consummate six words of advice on your road to fame and fortune: *When you got it – flaunt it!*

92.
Why I resent being called the "Original Mad Man" (and why, if you "get it," you have a shot at following in my footsteps).

In the very first week of 1960, at the time the *Mad Men* TV series is based, I started Papert Koenig Lois, the second creative agency in the world, inspiring and triggering what is revered today as the Advertising Creative Revolution. The 1960s was a heroic age in the history of the art of communication – the audacious movers and shakers of those times bear no resemblance to the cast of characters in *Mad Men*. This maddening show is nothing more than a soap opera, set in a glamorous office where stylish fools hump their appreciative, coiffured secretaries, suck up martinis, and smoke themselves to death as they produce dumb, lifeless advertising – oblivious to the inspiring Civil Rights movement, the burgeoning Women's Lib movement, the evil Vietnam War, and other seismic changes during the turbulent, roller-coaster 1960s that altered America forever.

The more I think about Mad Men, the more I take the show as a personal insult. So, fuck you Mad Men – you phony, "Gray Flannel Suit," male-chauvinist, no-talent, WASP, white-shirted, racist, anti-semitic, Republican SOBs!

Besides, when I was in my 30s I was better-looking than Don Draper.

JON HAMM
AS DON DRAPER

GEORGE LOIS
AS GEORGE LOIS
(1964)

93.
If you act like one of those lecherous TV Mad Men in your office, *you'll* wind up getting screwed.

Behave like a professional with dignity and self-discipline: Save your passion to drive your creative career, and keep your mind on your work. Nobody loves a womanizer, and nobody wants to work with an associate who's got one eye on his work and the other on a coworker's curves. It's the fastest, and ultimately the nastiest way to destroy a budding career.

94.
The only thing that gets better when it gets bigger is a penis.

All businesses founded by passionate entrepreneurs depend on constant creativity to achieve growth and success. But be aware that the bigger any enterprise gets, the more departments, the more marketing research, the more acquisitions, the more mergers, the more group grope, the more analysis paralysis (see 25, 26) – the worse the product becomes: lost creative control, lost passion, lost belief that you're producing greatness. And, as I predicted in the early 1970s, the more I witness "creative" ad agencies' work go downhill (through growth, merger, and acquisition) the more I know it's true: Big is worse, small is better.

Energy begets energy.

Workaholics are always asked why we work the way we do. It's got less to do with the work ethic and the drive to succeed than with motor movement. John Irving said it best in his novel, *The World According to Garp*, "Energy begets energy." When you're physically wiped out, motor movement produces adrenaline for the mind and body. For me, the war games of combative exercise for the body (I'm still playing full-contact basketball) and intellectual exercise for the mind (I'm still obsessively playing chess) is an essential part of my lifestyle. I believe sports and the intense intellectualism of the game of chess help drive and sustain the creative ethos. It's never too late to at least work out, and if you've never experienced the perfect calculus of chess, consider Thomas Huxley's Creationist conception of it: "The chessboard is the world, the pieces are the phenomena of the universe, the rules of the game are what we call the laws of Nature."

96.

The first owner of the Marlboro company died of lung cancer. So did the first *Marlboro Man*. Case closed.

When they were in their early 30s, I warned two great pals of mine who smoked like chimneys that they would die by the time they reached 50 years of age. They both, tragically, died in their 50th year of life. For the sake of your family, friends, and your career, if this call-out to you can influence you to end your suicidal path, I'd have done much more than mentor you on your way to a brilliant career. Keep up smoking and you'll experience The Big Sleep, way before your time.

P.S. I suppose I should look back at the logo I designed for the Indonesian Tobacco Co. with regret (see 79).

STAUNTON CHESS SET,
NATHANIEL COOK
(NAMED AFTER ENGLISH CHESS MASTER
HOWARD STAUNTON), 1849

97.
When you meet your mate, don't let her (him) get away. (Your creative juices will flow forever.)

On my first day at Pratt, I spotted Rosemary Lewandowski, a second generation Polish-American, who had come to New York City from Syracuse, N.Y., to build an artistic career and meet cultured people. Instead, she met me. I saw her face, and after a lo-o-o-ng check of her legs, I knew she was the woman who would be at my side the rest of my life. For 60 years she has loved me, fed me, raised our kids, nurtured our grandchildren, was one of the few female art directors of her time, has a career as a dynamic easel painter, and sees (and okays) everything I produce and then some — working with me as a thinker and copywriter on work I usually take credit for.

Having a mate who understands and contributes mightily to your ethos of life and work is a blessing beyond measure.

GEORGE AND ROSIE
10 MINUTES AFTER THEY FIRST MET
AT PRATT INSTITUTE IN 1949

A single day without work panics me. How about you?

In these bad days of mounting unemployment, I realize I have never been out of work a day in my life. Since I was six years old, my place was in my father's florist shop, at the end of each school day, including Saturdays and Sundays. I delivered flowers, cleaned, painted, watered, pruned, wrapped, hustled. I worked at anything my father needed me to do. I worked full-tilt every day to help sustain my family. Since my first job in advertising in 1950, right up until today, the very idea of a single day going by without "doing my job" absolutely panics me. So hop out of bed each day thrilled about the prospects of doing great work.

Attack every day as if it's your last.

99.
Don't sleep your life away.

I've always had the gnawing perception of sleep as a terrible enemy, one that robs each human being of a third of his time to work. What an 80-year-old man has done with his 233,600 hours awake is what gives meaning to his life. So if you're 20, and you live until you're 80, and if you sleep just one hour less each day – you could be awake and productive $2^{1/2}$ years more than your dozing competition! So if you sleep eight hours a day, train yourself to sleep seven! If you sleep seven hours a day, train yourself to sleep six! If you sleep six hours a day...well, you get the point. And if you're like me, sleep only three hours a day. (I've been awake more hours than any human being alive.)

GEORGE LOIS WITH HIS FATHER,
HARALAMBOS LOIS, IN FRONT
OF THE FAMILY FLORIST SHOP
IN THE BRONX, 1972

I would feel unarmed attacking a day of creative thinking if I hadn't read *The New York Times* early that morning.

My creative influences come from an eclectic brew, drawn from Bronx schoolyards, baseball lingo, comic strips, *Daily News* headlines, Marx Brothers movies, FDR speeches, popular songs, and other such mass cultural sources. I divided my teenage school years between delivering flowers, playing basketball, drawing, constructing model airplanes, visiting art galleries and museums –

"All the News That's Fit to Print"

The New Y

VOL. CLX ... No. 55,394

© 2011 The New York Times

NEW YORK, TU

BEHIND THE HUN

The Raid

Osama bin Laden, three other men and a woman were killed during a 40-minute raid by the United States Navy Seals on the outskirts of Abbottabad, Pakistan early Monday.

Bin Laden and his family had occupied the second and third floors of the **main building**, the last area to be cleared by American forces. He was killed in the latter part of the battle.

Residents burned their own trash here.

GATED ENTRANCE

and finally came to the realization in my late teens that an hour spent each morning reading *The New York Times* kept me informed on, and inspired by, the zeitgeist of the times (pun intended). Radio, television, and the internet can't come close to the visceral, informative, investigative, and analytical power of the world's great newspapers – *The Times* (London), *Le Monde, El Mundo*, etc. For you young generation of techies, reading in-depth journalism in a great newspaper beats the unedited, non-fact-checking bloggers every day of the week. **And, if you concentrate on every read, there are inspirations sprinkled throughout the paper.**

rk **Times**

MAY 3, 2011 $2.00

FOR BIN LADEN

7-foot-high
privacy wall

Clues Slowly Led to Location of Qaeda Chief

13-FOOT WALL

*This article is by **Mark Mazzetti, Helene Cooper** and **Peter Baker.***

101.
If you're a man, and you still think a woman can't compete with you, she's about to blindside you, pal.

Jack Nicholson famously said, "These days, women are better hung than the men." In the days before the Women's Liberation movement, men totally ruled in art direction and design — but women have come a long way, baby. Before the Advertising Creative Revolution in the 1960s, a few bravely fought the system (Cipe Pineles and Reba Sochis), but there have been many superb female art directors since then, including: Ruth Ansel, Bea Feitler, Louise Fili, Janet Froelich, Maira Kalman, Nancy Rice, and Paula Scher. These days, if you're a female with talent (and if you've got balls), the opportunities as a graphic designer, architect, film director, fashion designer, interior designer, etc., are more abundant than ever.

102.
If you're reading this and you're approaching 50 years of age, remember that oak trees do not produce acorns until they are 50 years old.

Charles Darwin was 50 when he wrote *On The Origin of Species*.

At 52, Ray Kroc, a milkshake-machine salesman, turned McDonald's from a small chain of restaurants into a humongous fast-food empire.

Colonel Sanders was in his 60s when he started KFC.

Dr. Ruth Westheimer became famous for her straight talk about sex when she was 52.

Louise Nevelson was in her 50s when she sold her first sculpture.

A New York public school teacher, Frank McCourt, at 66, wrote *Angela's Ashes* and a year later won a Pulitzer Prize.

Julia Child was just shy of 50 when she wrote her first cookbook.

A.C. Bhaktivedanta Swami Prabhupada founded the Hare Krishna movement when he was 69, with $7 to his name.

Hark the words of Samuel Beckett, reflecting on his own career when he intoned,
**"Ever tried. Ever Failed. No matter.
Try again. Fail again. Fail better."**

103.
Never act cocky.
(But you better be cocksure!)

Big difference. If you're cocky, you're a big-mouth.
If you're cocksure, you're a confident creative! Never act cocky
unless you're Muhammad Ali (who said the morning
after he became heavyweight champion of the world: "A rooster
crows only when it sees light—put him in the dark
and he'll never crow—I have seen the light and I'm crowing!")
But there's only one Ali. As a creative, you must have
the talent and confidence to be cocksure that your concepts
are memorable—with the power to produce
cause and effect change.
If you're a business entrepreneur,
you must exude confidence.
And if you're in a creative
industry, you must be
dead certain what your
work can accomplish
for your client, and
promise that it
will do just that!
(If you don't have
the balls to promise,
you'll never be great.)

104.
Learn to write one singular, coherent, informative, insightful, spectacular sentence to replace your illiterate, off-the-cuff twittering!

THIS SENTENCE IS UNDER 140 CHARACTERS IN LENGTH, AS PER TWITTER REQUIREMENTS

Twitter less, think more.
And how about using proper English
in your emails, for a change?!
(Write everything, do everything, as well
as it can be done.)

105.
Or better yet, stop tweeting your life away and do something productive: Learn to draw!

An idea can be communicated better with a drawing (so if you can't draw, learn). For anyone whose passion is to spend their lifetime as a painter, or sculptor, architect, film director, graphic designer, fashion designer, product designer, set designer, interior decorator, inventor, or even an entrepreneur, if you can't express an idea in a drawing, it means you can't *see*. Even a *passable* sketch dramatically helps crystallize an idea. So, if you can't draw, make it a daily project and learn. It will not only make you a profoundly better communicator of your ideas, it will add more joy to the way you see.

ONE OF MILLIONS OF DRAWINGS
FOR PROPOSED PHOTOGRAPHS FOR ADS
BY GEORGE LOIS (IN 1986, OF
TOMMY HILFIGER, WITH THE HEADLINE
WHAT MAKES TOMMY RUN?)

You cannot teach a crab to walk straight.

106.

A crab is a crab, a snake is a snake, and in the everyday experience of your creative life, a fool is a fool. When your instincts identify those who are unmoved by the ambition of Big Idea creativity, whether it's an employer or a client, reject them and walk straight out the door.

107.
Don't get mad, get even (?!).

In the *Merchant of Venice*, Shakespeare has Shylock saying:
If you prick us, do we not bleed? If you tickle us, do we not laugh?
If you poison us, do we not die? And if you wrong us, shall we not
revenge? I disagree with Shylock. Here's what I think:
Fuggedaboutit! Don't let your tormentors distract you from your
destiny. If you keep chewing it over, they win, you lose.
So don't sue, don't bitch, and don't lose sight of where you're headed!

P.S. However, whenever I spot an obituary of somebody
on my shit-list, I hold up the paper to show my wife and snarl,
"I told you I'd get the son-of-a-bitch."

108.
"Then why the fuck didn't you make it that way in the first place!"

The most convincing lesson to everyone in the human race was given to me in 1960 by the restaurateur Joe Baum. The pioneering crusader in converting eating in America into a theatrical and aesthetic experience was welcoming me as his advertising guru. At the bar of his spectacular Forum of the Twelve Caesars, Baum checked to see if I was watching his every move as he ordered a Bloody Mary. Before sipping his drink, he asked the bartender,

"Is this the *best* Bloody Mary you can make?"

"Yes, Mr. Baum," the bartender answered with assurance.

"Taste it," Baum ordered.

The bartender sipped and reflected.

"It's delicious," he decided.

"Can you make a *better* one?" asked Baum. The bartender mixed a new Bloody Mary.

"Now taste this one and tell me what you think," said Baum. The bartender took a sip.

"This is *very* good, Mr. Baum. *It's perfect!*"

"Then why the fuck didn't you make it that way in the first place?" barked the great Joe Baum.

Remember this story every time you do anything in life, including sweeping the floor and washing the dishes.

109.
If you don't work loosey-goosey, you're a dead duck.

When I was in my early 20s, a leading couturier told me that creating a fashion line was a terrible everyday working experience — "sheer hell," were his words. I sarcastically offered the advice that he quit and take a job as a longshoreman — I've met plenty of hard-working men and women who take pride in their work, do it to the best of their ability, and do it with a smile on their face. Working hard demands that you laugh a lot or you turn into a drone and your work shows it. In any creative industry, to be creative, the vital juices must flow, unimpeded, with as little anxiety as possible in coming up with idea after idea. I like the phrase loosey-goosey to describe the kind of ambience so essential to me as I go about my work with gusto and pleasure. I like to have people around me who smile a lot, and laugh at will, and are smart enough to get my puns. Fun in creating is the fun of living, and should permeate and shape every aspect of working with others. In so many ways, **the love of life, the sublime joy of living and working, must pervade every aspect of your work.**

110.
Work comfortably (as you can see) in a formal setting.

Most people work *formally* in a *comfortable* setting. (The world is made up of people who insist that they want to exist in a "lived-in" atmosphere. I say it's a rationalization for being a slob.) I love *people* informality in a structured, precise surrounding.

GEORGE LOIS, 1973

People acting loosey-goosey (see 109) makes for an atmosphere where you can think creatively and share those thoughts without being accused of saying something inane or stupid. Besides, I don't think I've ever created a Big Idea wearing a suit and tie.

111.
Make your surroundings
a metaphor for who you are.

I once visited a great architect in his office and was shocked
by the clutter and tastelessness of his surroundings.
How unlike his office were the structures and environment
he produced! He spent his lifetime striving to make
the world outside him look harmonious, while he looked at
a mess inside the very room where he did his work.

The only thing I ever permit on my desk is the job I'm working on.
And, in my work place, there is nothing on the walls
(except my nineteenth-century Seth Thomas clock) to distract me
from what I'm supposed to be thinking about on my desk.
I've always invested so much effort in my immediate surroundings
because the objects and surfaces and forms that
surround me must feel aesthetically right to me. Your working
surroundings should not be a presentation to your
clients. (Indeed, when my clients first see my office they invariably
give me a strange look.)

**Everything I believe in is reflected in this photograph
of my work area: precision, simplicity, clarity.**

And your home should *not* be a presentation to your friends.
Surroundings should relate to who you are,
what you love, and to what you deem important in life.

112.
We all need heroes.
Mine is Paul Rand, an iconoclast who made it big in a constipated business world.

Paul Rand stands at the very pinnacle of my graphic forefathers. Cantankerous, irascible, loving – bristling with talent, brimming over with taste, and endowed with invincible personal conviction – the original and badass Rand showed the way. His fresh, pioneering work first appeared in 1938, and when I entered high school in 1945, the 31-year-old Rand had already acquired international stature, accelerated by his 1947 book *Thoughts on Design*, which takes an honored place in my extensive library. Now a tattered bible, I read and reread it a thousand times in my early teens. Paul Rand's war against the mediocrity in the design world created an absolute supreme standard for the rest of my life, as I have attempted to build on the mastery of what came before. When the Pratt Institute Gallery (in Brooklyn) was inaugurated in 1985, honoring Pratt's most important students with a two-man exhibition entitled *Paul Rand & George Lois, The Great Communicators*, it was a young boy's dream come true.
I stand resolutely on his broad shoulders.

PAUL RAND AND HIS EYE BEE M POSTER
BASED ON HIS IBM LOGO (1981)

113.
Extoll your Mentors.

When the world deems you "a success," always, always,
recognize your mentors (if you claim you had none,
you're an ungrateful liar). I had a lot of breaks in my life,
including being raised in a hard-working Greek
family and marrying the right woman, but three people
recognized my talent and led me to what I do today.
I speak about them often in my lectures, and in my books.
Years from now, when you become a hot-shot,
speak passionately about your mentors. May you be
as blessed as I have been.

IDA ENGLE

My drawings at P.S. 7 caught the eye
of my seventh-grade art teacher,
Mrs. Engel, who handed me a black,
stringed portfolio filled with my
drawings, which she had saved, and
sent me to the High School of
Music & Art (a brilliant school founded
in 1936 by Mayor Fiorello LaGuardia)
for an all-day entrance exam.
When I was enthusiastically accepted,
I knew that I would never
be a florist.

HERSCHEL LEVIT

I suffered through my first year at Pratt because it was an unsophisticated rehash of my formative years at the High School of Music & Art. But after a few months of my second year, Herschel Levit, a bow-tied, aesthete design teacher, jump-started my career by sending me to Reba Sochis' design studio. Mr. Levit inspired 31 years of Pratt students, and amazingly, seven of his student protégés have been inducted into the Art Directors Club Hall of Fame: Steve Frankfurt, Bob Giraldi, Steve Horn, George Lois, Sheila Metzner, Stan Richards, and Len Sirowitz.

REBA SOCHIS

The greatest day of my professional life was when I met Reba Sochis— a great designer, a great dame, a great curser. The loveliest lady in the world of design (with a nose more crooked than mine) was the first of the modernist designers I worked with who were inducted into the Art Directors Club Hall of Fame (joining Bill Golden, Herb Lubalin, Bill Bernbach, and Bob Gage). One week out of Pratt, when I cashed my first paycheck, I couldn't believe I was actually being paid to refine my craft in her queendom of perfectionism.

114.
Creating advertising that is icon rather than con depends on the deep belief that your message is more than the purchase of a product or service.

In 1961, Dr. Benjamin Spock asked me to do a New York subway poster. Nuclear testing in the atmosphere by the U.S. and the Soviet Union was threatening the continuation of life on our planet, without one bomb being dropped in the Cold War conflict. Dr. Spock, one of the brave leaders of the Committee for a Sane Nuclear Policy (SANE), alerted the public with warnings by Nobel scientists that the fallout from radioactive materials would result in a growing number of birth defects and deaths.

The poster combined the image of a pregnant woman with a hard-hitting, absolutely factual headline. The press called me a commie sympathizer. Today, nearly a half century after the Nuclear Test Ban Treaty of 1963, it seems incomprehensible that a poster about the malignant peril of nuclear fallout could ever have sparked such outrage. But my poster made an iconic statement that opened the eyes of many in those scary days.

If you don't believe that advertising can be Icon rather than Con, you'll never understand the potential of great creativity.

1¼ Million unborn children will be born dead or have some gross defect because of Nuclear Bomb testing

SANE

WHEN I SENT ANDY WARHOL THE ISSUE OF *ESQUIRE* WITH HIM DROWNING
IN HIS OWN SOUP, THE BE-WIGGED ONE BEGGED ME TO TRADE THE ORIGINAL ART FOR
ONE OF HIS CAMPBELL'S SOUP CAN PAINTINGS (WORTH MULTI-MILLIONS TODAY).
BUT I TOLD ANDY THAT ONE DAY I WOULD DONATE THE ORIGINAL ART
TO MoMA—AND IN 2008, I DID.

115.
Is what we do Art?

Creativity in advertising and graphic design, as I practice it, is art. My professional practice derives directly from romantic ideas of the superhuman artist. I insist on the inviolability of my graphic work, all created with an ethos of allegiance to art rather than science, even though they powerfully serve a commercial purpose. I *am* an artist – and as it has thrillingly been for artists in the twentieth century, outrage is the dynamic practice of my career. The great creative personality is the archetype of the nonorganization man, and defying convention in spectacular ways should be the driving force of the life of the entrepreneur and all of us who work in a creative industry. **If you're talented and passionate enough, you too will create Art!**

116.
You're at your happiest when you're creating.

You continually read about creative people who speak of the "pain and torment" of the creative process. Huh? They and I live in two different worlds. When your mind is constantly in action, the visceral feeling of search and enlightenment becomes addictive, as important to your sustenance as sex, food, and drink.
The joy of the creative process, digging and aspiring for an answer, becomes euphoric when you finally get the Big Idea.
That joy of the creative process, minute by minute, hour after hour, day by day, is the sublime path to true happiness.

Happy people work harder.
Work should ennoble, not kill, the human spirit,
so we must labor, not for profit, but for perfection.
(However, $aints are as deserving
of the good things in life as $inners.)

GEORGE LOIS, 2010

117.
You'll never be the creative person you aspire to be if you don't know where it all came from.

In 1972, as president of the prestigious Art Directors Club of New York, I founded the Art Directors Hall of Fame and we inaugurated the first eight giants of the design world – innovators and conceptual thinkers who laid the groundwork for those of us who followed to become the modern and meaningful art directors and graphic communicators of our time. The selection each year since then not only informs young people aspiring to be designers, copywriters, photographers, illustrators, product designers, etc., but also serves significantly as an imperative source of inspiration. By the year 2012, 166 men and women from around the world had gained this highest Lifetime Achievement Award. All lived their lives as art directors, salespeople, thinkers, and innovators, but most of all – artists.

As George Santayana wrote, "Those who cannot remember the past, are condemned to repeat it."
You can't create the future without knowing what came before it.

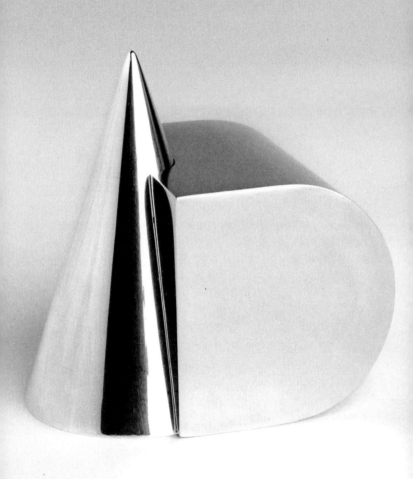

THE A.D. HALL OF FAME AWARD: AN INTERACTIVE "A"
(IN THE SHAPE OF A CONE) AND A MOVEABLE "D"
(THAT FITS AROUND THE CONE),
DESIGNED BY GEORGE LOIS AND GENE FEDERICO, 1972

118.

"If you do it right, it will live forever."

MASSIMO VIGNELLI, DESIGNER

In the mid-1960s, Massimo Vignelli and I, both in our early 30s, were well aware of and admirers of each others work.
In a discussion about our approach to design, Vignelli summed up the ethos of his life by saying, "George, if you do it right, it will live forever." Almost 50 years later, the legendary graphic, interior, and product designer, along with Lella, his lifelong wife and partner, cut the ribbon and officially opened the magnificent Vignelli Center for Design Studies at the Rochester Institute of Technology, designed by him and dedicated to fostering studies related to the acquisition of the archives of the modern masters of design.

Among my work in the Vignelli Center Collection is my 1968 *Esquire* cover depicting the three most mourned Americans since FDR. An idealized, saintlike John F. Kennedy, Robert F. Kennedy, and Dr. Martin Luther King, Jr., are resurrected and hauntingly watch over Arlington Cemetery, in a dreamlike epitaph on the murder of American goodness. Massimo Vignelli was right: Do it right, and it will live forever.

35th Anniversary Issue of
Esquire
Salvaging the 20th Century

OCTOBER 1968
$1⁵⁰

"GEORGE LOIS' ICONIC *ESQUIRE* COVERS CHRONICLE A CRITICAL PERIOD
OF AMERICAN SOCIAL AND POLITICAL TURMOIL AND THE LEGACY OF A REMARKABLE
GRAPHIC DESIGNER AND COMMUNICATOR."

THE NEW YORK TIMES

119.

"A great deal of talent is lost to the world for want of a little courage."

SYDNEY SMITH, BRITISH WRITER

One of the most thrilling pages in Webster's Dictionary zeroes in on the meaning of the word "courage": *marked by bold resolution in withstanding the dangerous, alarming or difficult...a firmness of spirit that faces danger or extreme difficulty without flinching or retreating...an ability to hold one's own and fight for one's principles.* A talented but meek creative personality can never join the pantheon of the greats, because timidity leads to mediocrity. Fear of the fray results in "a great deal of talent lost to the world."

The courage to create only superb work, through thick and thin, and fight to protect it at all cost, is not generated in the head...
it comes from your very heart and soul.

OF THE NUMEROUS PROFESSIONAL AWARDS I'VE RECEIVED, THE ONE I VALUE MOST IS THIS
KING GEORGE V WWI MEDAL DEPICTING SAINT GEORGE SLAYING THE DRAGON, LOVINGLY PRESENTED
TO ME BY MY COLLEAGUES AT LOIS PITTS GERSHON IN 1979, ON THE FIRST ANNIVERSARY
OF THE DEATH OF MY 20-YEAR-OLD SON, HARRY JOE, WITH THE INSCRIPTION "A MEDAL TO OUR
UNDAUNTED LEADER." IT WAS GIVEN TO ME IN RECOGNITION OF SOLDIERING ON,
CONTINUING TO CREATE THE VERY BEST IN ADVERTISING, WITH WHAT WILLIAM WORDSWORTH CALLED,
"HEART AND BUOYANT SPIRIT IN THE FACE OF AN INEXPLICABLE TRAGEDY."

120.
You are the master of your fate:
you are the captain of your soul.

With all the lucky breaks, or unhappily, the bad breaks one endures,
I believe a person still decides their own fate, that they ordain
what kind of family life they have, what they believe in, and what
kind of work they produce. You *can* decide that no-one can
make you produce bad work! The Abominable No-Men, the philistines
of the business world abound. But if you've got the right stuff,
"they" can't stop you from following your bliss, they can't keep you
from demonstrating your talent, and they can't stop you
from fulfilling your destiny. Never.

While incarcerated at
Robben Island and
Pollsmoor prisons for 27 years,
Nelson Mandela,
the legendary South African
anti-apartheid activist,
recited *Invictus* (Latin for
"unconquered"), the iconic poem
written in 1875 by the English
poet William Ernest Henley,
to his fellow prisoners,
empowering all with its message
of self-mastery.

Out of the night that covers me,
Black as the pit from pole to pole,
I thank whatever gods may be
For my unconquerable soul.

In the fell clutch of circumstance
I have not winced nor cried aloud.
Under the bludgeonings of chance
My head is bloody, but unbowed.

Beyond this place of wrath and tears
Looms but the Horror of the shade,
And yet the menace of the years
Finds and shall find me unafraid.

It matters not how strait the gate,
How charged with punishments the scroll,
I am the master of my fate:
I am the captain of my soul.

**Among the greatest pioneers
of modern graphic design are:**

Dr. Mehemed Fehmy Agha
Saul Bass
Herbert Bayer
Lester Beall
Alexey Brodovitch
A. M. Cassandre
William Golden
Alexander Liberman
Raymond Loewy
Herbert Matter
Irving Penn
Paul Rand
Bradbury Thompson

The greatest of my contemporaries are:

Ivan Chermayeff
Lou Dorfsman
Gene Federico
Bob Gage
Bob Gill
Helmut Krone
Herb Lubalin
Tony Palladino
Bill Taubin
Massimo Vignelli
Henry Wolf
Fred Woodward

I proudly dedicate this book to these 25 master communicators.

Many thanks to Amanda Renshaw for sparking
the creation of this book,
and Victoria Clarke for her superb editing.

And love and appreciation to my son Luke Lois,
who designed this book by my side.